The Medusa Enigma

The Medusa Enigma

Dino Panvini, M.D.

Library of Congress Control Number: 2019900699
ISBN: Hardcover   978-1-7960-1125-8
                   Softcover   978-1-7960-1124-1
                   eBook   978-1-7960-1123-4

Print information available on the last page.

Rev. date: 02/18/2019

To order additional copies of this book, contact:
Xlibris
1-888-795-4274
www.Xlibris.com
Orders@Xlibris.com
785778

CONTENTS

PREFACE

Everything you are about to read is true. Although you may think this is a work of fiction, it is not! This book will take you deep inside the corruption of the United States' legal and medical systems, and how it led to my near-death experience and multiple attempts on my life.

My name is Dr. Dino Panvini, MD, FACS. I am an American-born, board-certified urologist with more than thirty years' experience in urology. I have held administrative positions as chairman of surgery and chairman of urology in several US hospitals. I come from a long line of doctors, dating back to the fifteenth century in Italy. I started my clinical practice in New York City in 1987 and ultimately ended up in Fort Mohave, Arizona, in 2010. I am a Diplomate of the American Board of Urology, a Fellow of the American College of Surgeons, and a Fellow of the International College of Surgeons, and I have been fellowship trained in integrative medicine.

In thirty years, I have never had a malpractice judgment or settlement against me, something few surgeons in this country can say. As you will learn, one of the lawyers mentioned in this book filed malicious, fraudulent malpractice actions against me for the same case three times, repeatedly alleging that I murdered my patient—despite having no evidence at all.

You will learn about my near-death experience and multiple attempts on my life, the corruption within the judicial system, and a bizarre divorce like none you have ever encountered.

The legal and medical corruption at work in the United States is a contagion—an epidemic that affects every American citizen, in one way or another, every day. Lawyers are not policed by the American Bar Association, and they run rampant, injuring millions of Americans financially, emotionally, and professionally. The legal system needs a complete overhaul, which only Americans can do. Freedom of the press provides us with a way of alerting the general public, which is our constitutional right under the First Amendment.

Many people reading my words may have experienced similar situations, but none to the extent that I have. My story reveals the complete abuse of the legal system by lawyers, against not only doctors but also ordinary Americans from all walks of life. It is time that Americans take back their rights by demanding that the federal government police the legal system and prevent lawyers from taking malicious actions like the ones you will read about here.

Because I am discussing actual events, I have changed the names of many characters to avoid further litigation. These are dangerous people, as you will see.

I hope you enjoy this true story. You will find it to be suspenseful and dramatic, but the warnings I offer about the danger to American society are as real as the things that happened to me.

CHAPTER ONE

Death's Doorstep

Am I really going to die like this? I wondered. *Immobilized and crushed to death under boxes in my own bedroom, with no way to contact the outside world?*

I felt as if I had come to the end of my story, and to be honest, many people would have been relieved to arrive at that point. By May 2015, when I had the accident that nearly cost me my life, I had already been traveling down some of the darkest paths imaginable for nearly fifteen years. I had lost my wife, children, and business, and I had been threatened to the point that I was forced to flee the country. In the process of achieving medical breakthroughs and saving countless lives, I had made deadly enemies. Just when it seemed as if I was about to make a fresh start, it looked as though my life might be over.

For thirty years, I have been a urologic surgeon. I completed my general surgery training at a hospital in Brooklyn, New

York, and a Yale University–affiliated hospital in Connecticut. In 1987, after doing graduate work at the urologic surgery program at a university in the Midwest, I began my career in New York City, where I maintained three offices in Queens and Manhattan. After the events of 9/11, I decided to seek a change and spent the 2000s in private practice in Indiana, Nevada, and Arizona. While working in Sparks, Nevada, and Fort Mojave, Arizona, I built up my practices to offer the best urology treatments in the western United States, frequently seeing patients who had traveled from several states away to seek my expertise. However, the chaos and threats against my life and livelihood eventually became too much, and I was forced to move to Italy.

After living and working in Italy for some time, I moved to a resort city in Florida. When I left Italy, I had placed all my possessions into containers to be shipped to the United States. With international shipping, it took months for everything to arrive.

In Florida, I rented a beautiful house near the water, just twenty-five minutes' drive from the hospital where I planned to work. But the house was empty and I had no furniture, so I slept on an inflatable mattress on the floor, which was not the best thing for my back.

On May 19, 2015, the day of the accident that nearly took my life, I had driven from New Orleans to my home in Florida. I had been attending the American Urological Association's annual conference in New Orleans. The drive from Florida to Louisiana had been beautiful. I had kept my car's sunroof open so I could soak up UV rays on my face and get some vitamin D. As a busy doctor, I kept such long hours that I looked as pale as a vampire, even though I lived in the Sunshine State.

The GPS took me right to the front door of my hotel, which was within walking distance of the Memorial Convention Center. I checked into my room and then walked over to collect my badge and the list of lectures and courses. As a member of the American Urological Association, I had registered online, so the procedure was smooth and easy.

The event ran four full days, May 12 2015, allowing me to learn about the latest updates in urology, take several courses to keep my medical knowledge current, and learn about new treatment procedures and methods. I had attended annual meetings in New Orleans many times, but that was my first time there since Hurricane Katrina had nearly destroyed the beautiful city in 2005.

After checking into the hotel, I spent the rest of the day relaxing, enjoying the city, and preparing to attend lectures and courses. It seems that I took thirty hours of credit courses during those five days. I say "it seems" because, as a result of the events I am about to describe, I have no memory of the conference or anything else relating to my trip to New Orleans. Everything I have just told you has been reconstructed from hotel bills, emails from the AUA, Continuing Medical Education (CME) credits, and other outside sources.

When I got back home to Florida, Sofia Lombardi, a friend at the time, was nowhere to be found. It seemed likely to me that she was doing something with her son, Dick Lombardi, but whatever it was, I didn't want to know about it. Dick was trouble and always had been. He was a drug user and a thief, and I wouldn't allow him in the house. I had too many valuable possessions, including a collection of gold coins. Sofia had been spending time with him while I was busy with my medical professional obligations.

So there I was at home in Florida, all alone after spending a week in intense study at a medical conference. To relax and decompress a little, I decided to sort through some boxes that contained medical books and framed diplomas. Stored in the bedroom, they were part of the shipment that had recently arrived from Italy, but I hadn't had time to open them or find places to put them. The garage, too, was full of boxes awaiting distribution and sorting.

What happened next was related to the stress I was under, with the constant, malicious actions of lawyers and their fraudulent legal maneuvers against me. As a type two diabetic, I took a weekly injection. On the day I was due for my shot, I frequently felt slightly disoriented and got a headache, especially if I had been doing hard, physical labor such as moving of heavy boxes. The stress of all my legal troubles also would have raised my glucose levels.

As I attempted to move the boxes, I must have suffered one of these moments of disorientation, and I lost control.

The boxes toppled and fell on me, forcing me into a contorted position on my bedroom floor. The boxes under me twisted my back, while those on top of me pinned my legs so that I could not move them. I tried desperately to free myself, struggling to lift the boxes off my legs, but to no avail. Lying on the floor, I felt my pain grow with each passing moment and dizziness overtake me. My mind became foggy and I couldn't think clearly, but I knew that I was in real trouble.

My legs were totally immobilized. I could not reach my bed or get to the bathroom, though both were just steps away and easily accessible under normal circumstances. The muscles of my legs were crushed, sending toxic substances into my bloodstream where they were absorbed by my kidneys, causing massive trauma and eventual acute kidney failure.

I lay there, trapped and in pain, for several days. I got a cell phone call from Sofia, but the specifics are lost to me. I am a proud Italian man and do not like to ask for help unless it is absolutely necessary, but I didn't realize the gravity of my situation. I learned later that the call was just five minutes long. I also got a call from her mother, but what she said and how I reacted to it are gone, just like my entire trip to New Orleans. I lost memory from months of my life and very nearly lost my life.

Before my trip to New Orleans I had unfinished business to attend to with my new professional career change. Dr. Abdul Nassif, the associate who recruited me, was an unmarried Pakistani. Short, thin, and muscular, he had a dark complexion and a follicular deficiency of the head and face. Always well dressed, he was a charming man with a talent for persuading people to agree with him. I later learned that he had obsessive compulsive disorder as well. On the day before my trip to New Orleans (Tuesday, May 11, 2015), I had met with him in my new office in Panama City, Florida.

Dr. Nassif had earlier persuaded me to return to the United States from Italy and brought me in to set up and run a new urological division of his medical practice, Florida Resort City Radiation Oncology. The contracts governing my employment agreement had been signed months earlier, in January 2015. But I had brought a large amount of medical equipment and supplies with me—from catheters and biopsy needles to a hydraulic examination table, urodynamic tables and equipment, and trans-rectal ultrasound equipment—and we needed to establish definitive terms so that I would be reimbursed for use of this equipment.

I was to be paid $6,000 a month for it, but Dr. Nassif was already three months behind, which troubled me. He had been using my equipment and supplies without paying me, and I could see that this situation would only continue to escalate and agitate me as word got around about my success rate and the practice grew.

I had been performing in-office surgical procedures—cystoscopies and vasectomies—using trans-rectal ultrasound guided biopsy, which involved inserting a special probe into the patient's rectum after it had been anesthetized and then probing any suspicious areas. With the patient lying on his side, I would identify the prostate, take measurements, and then insert the needle through a guide port to take biopsies under ultrasound guidance. If cancer was detected, it could then be treated either through surgery or radiation therapy.

Nassif and I had frequent disagreements on how to treat prostate cancer. He was interested only in radiating prostate cancer, rather than surgical extirpation, and we argued about it often. He would say, "You don't understand! I hired you to find the prostate cancers so that I can treat them with radiation!" He tried to deter me from performing surgery for prostate cancer, not for medical reasons but because radiation therapy earned him $25,000 in profit, as opposed to $1,800 for surgery. Surgery is curative, however, unlike radiation.

By the time I joined the cancer center, I had already identified about a dozen men with prostate cancer. Some of these patients needed surgery, but I was having difficulty getting admitting privileges at local hospitals. I had been battling a lawyer who had fraudulently sued me three times, falsely alleging that I had murdered my own patient, and this information was available on the internet and damaging my reputation. A group of urologic physicians in the area, headed by Dr. Luis Perez, was concerned about the competition I represented, but they saw an opening with the malpractice lawsuits and all the other crap that was on the internet about me.

My ex-wife had hired an attorney to file a fraudulent malpractice claim against me, alleging that I had murdered a patient, and this claim had been filed three times in state and federal courts. So this local group of urologic physicians had read about these fictitious allegations from the malpractice claims. They knew that I had talent and would probably eat into their profits, so they did everything possible to keep me from getting privileges at either of the local hospitals, where they were represented on the credentialing committees. They repeatedly asked for evidence that I had not murdered my patient—a preposterous allegation made by a bankruptcy attorney. How do you prove that something didn't happen?

Big monopolies of physicians and health care organizations tend to band together to prevent newcomers from coming into the community. I was a talented newcomer, but I was not welcome strictly for reasons of self-preservation and controlling the medical community. This particular group was represented on the medical executive committee and the credentialing committee, which made my application process for hospital licensure take longer than usual.

While I was having trouble getting into local hospitals to perform surgery on patients, I also was disturbed by Dr. Nassif's persistent attempts to coerce me into recommending *only* radiation therapy to patients. His insistence that I refer prostate cancer patients to him so that he could bill for the radiotherapy was unsettling to say the least. I found his approach of radiating all prostate cancers to be extremely unethical, since radiation therapy does not have the same cure rate as surgical extirpation in properly identified patients. But he didn't give a damn about the patients—he just wanted that $25,000.

Even before the hospital granted my operating room and admitting privileges, which were still pending, I was concerned about the practice that I was setting up. Just before I left for the conference in New Orleans, we finally finished all the paperwork—the contracts for employment and reimbursement for the disposable supplies and equipment I had brought from Italy. Once everything was signed, I placed my copy in my desk drawer and we shook hands. I should have listened to my gut, because the disputes between the two of us left me feeling uneasy. But I remained optimistic that things would improve and that I would soon be practicing medicine in the ethical manner in which I had conducted my entire career.

Little did I know what was to come.

CHAPTER TWO

The Psychopaths

As I lay immobilized on the floor of my bedroom in May 2015, I received a phone call from Sofia. She was in another state; she had mentioned going to Tennessee to spend time with her son while I was at the urologic convention in New Orleans. I didn't want to worry her by telling her I was trapped, because I'm a proud Italian man who doesn't like to disperse negative energy if I can contain the situation myself. I was still telling myself that I would soon find a way to get free. Later I learned that Sofia had also called her mother, Helen—the only other phone number she had committed to memory.

Helen then called to tell me that Sofia had been arrested! She didn't know much more than that; she couldn't tell me what state Miss Lombardi was in, only that she was in Fort Alexander County Jail. I didn't want to worry Helen by letting her know that I was trapped and unable to move or sit upright, so I just said that I would try to make arrangements to have her daughter bailed out.

I didn't know what state Fort Alexander County Jail was in either, and why had Sofia been arrested? But somehow my mind jumped past those questions and I went into immediate problem-solving mode like surgeons must sometimes do. Though I can't recall now how I did it, I found a bail bondsman, arranged for her release, and asked him to give her two hundred dollars in cash. The entire thing was paid for with one of her own credit cards, using a photo I had on my phone, which pulled from her checking account, so in essence she was bailing herself out.

When that was done, I texted Helen to let her know that Sofia would be released, and then I might have passed out. I should have had the presence of mind to call 911, but I just wasn't thinking clearly. In any case, my phone was dead by then.

I later learned that when the bail bondsman got Sofia out of jail, she was handed a small bag containing only the clothing she had been wearing at the time of her arrest. When she asked where the rest of her possessions were, she was told the rest would be held until the matter had been settled.

Without identification or money, Sofia knew she wouldn't be able to get a hotel room or buy food. Still the police department refused to return her personal property until her court date—June 5, nearly two weeks away. Meanwhile Sofia was left without her car, driver's license, medication, cash and credit cards, and suitcases containing additional clothes.

It was the bail bondsman who helped Sofia, checking both of them into a nearby hotel with the same credit card number that had been used for the bail. She told Sofia that she was free to go anywhere she liked, as long as she showed up for her hearing on June 5. Where Sofia went and what she did until then, with just two hundred dollars to her name, was up to her.

As soon as Sofia got into her hotel room, she began trying to call me, but my cell phone was dead—and by then I was likely unconscious to boot.

When I met Sofia Lombardi in Las Vegas in 2012, she was an intelligent, middle-aged woman. Thin but very attractive, she had dark black hair with a reddish hue. She had a successful medical equipment leasing company, and I was running a thriving urological practice in the nearby town of Fort Mojave, Arizona. We developed a friendship, and over time we became good friends.

I had thirteen people working for me in Arizona: a doctor, nurses, nurse practitioners, physicians' assistants, and techs. I was the biggest income generator at the local hospital, with patients traveling to see me from California, Las Vegas, Phoenix, and even farther away.

Unfortunately, there was another general surgeon in the area who was jealous of my success, which he felt made him look like a minion. Throughout this story, I will refer to him only as Dr. Morelli, and as you will see, the man is a dangerous psychopath. A short, pale, sickly looking balding man with a Napoleon complex, Dr. Morelli was very controlling and territorial, and he always wanted the spotlight to be on him. The operating room personnel didn't like him because he was extremely arrogant and mean; also his surgical skills were questionable, which caused his patients many complications. He wasn't handling any major cases at that time. In contrast, I was regularly performing surgical procedures that had never been done in that region. For example, when a cancer patient had their bladder removed, I made a new bladder out of part of their intestine. That kind of work intimidated him.

Morelli was a bitter, callous man with grandiose ideas about himself and a chip on his shoulder. He tried to terrify everyone around him, as if he enjoyed the stimulation of causing fear and terror. He exhibited no remorse or guilt when he would do something to jeopardize a staff member's professional career. He showed no emotion and had a total lack of empathy, which is symptomatic of a psychopath.

Dr. Morelli knew that I was also a herniologist who had written a chapter in the textbook *Hernia*. I'm known for performing hernia operations under local anesthesia, so that when the issue is resolved, the patient can simply rise from the table and walk away with little pain. Most surgeons, however, do this procedure under general anesthesia, which was what Dr. Morelli preferred. His patients had horrendous complications, including suffering severe groin pain from improperly situated mesh, as well as recurrences of their hernias.

When you employ local anesthesia, you can put the mesh into the location of the hernia and then have the patient cough to make sure proper containment has been achieved. If necessary, you can adjust the mesh, put sutures in, or do whatever else is necessary, and then close them up and have them walk from the operating table to the recovery room. You can't do that with a patient who's asleep, though. How can you get an unconscious person to cough?

As a result of Dr. Morelli's reliance on general anesthetic and his general incompetence, a number of his patients would come to me after being treated by him, but I always turned them away. I would tell them, "I'm not going to touch you, because you were operated on by Dr. Morelli, and I don't want any battles here." His feelings about me were obvious, and I didn't want to exacerbate the situation. I would recommend them to general surgeons in the Las Vegas area, but I never repaired his shoddy work myself.

There were times when we shared patients; for example, I would do a prostatectomy and he would do a colonoscopy on the same patient. But I never invaded his territory, and he couldn't invade mine because he wasn't a urologic surgeon.

Still, as time went by, Dr. Morelli and his wife, Margaret Morelli, seemed to be driven mad by my success. Determined to drive me out of town, they began to infiltrate my practice starting with my receptionist, Betty Washington, who handled the books, logged appointments, and did everything to keep the office running.

One day in 2012, Betty came into my office, said she was having a financial crisis, and asked if I could help her out.

I said, "You've been with me since the beginning. What's going on?"

Betty claimed that the IRS was auditing her and that she owed $50,000 in back taxes.

"Wow, fifty thousand," I replied. "That's a lot of money. Maybe I can help you out." I was doing well in the practice and she was helping—at least, I thought she was. So I lent her the $50,000, with the understanding that she was going to pay it back in either overtime or money.

Soon after I gave Betty the money, though, she claimed that she couldn't report to work because of corneal abrasions. I asked myself, *What kind of corneal abrasion? This is bullshit.* I had another staffer drive to Betty's house, and there she was holding a yard sale and exhibiting no signs of vision problems. She had lied to me, and it was obvious that she was in collusion with the doctors who were trying to undermine me, so I terminated her.

Of course, that created more problems, because I then had to defend my decision not to pay her unemployment benefits. Ultimately, Betty pursued her claim so far that I was forced to undergo a deposition, and guess who her star witness was? Margaret Morelli! That solidified everything in my mind. What did Margaret Morelli have to do with my office personnel? How could she have anything to say about my office employee issues when she knew nothing about them— or did she? Obviously Betty had conspired with Morelli to help bring down my office and destroy my professional career.

Person by person, the two of them then got rid of my key office personnel. Betty was the first strike. Before she left, she screwed up my appointment schedule so horribly that the office wasn't functional. She changed passwords to multiple computer programs and generally left everything in chaos. When I hired Mary to replace her, they went after her too. Mary began to receive threatening phone calls at home, warning her that if she continued to work for me, she would "never work for anybody again." It got so bad that Mary got spooked and quit.

Then they approached Maya, my nurse practitioner. I don't know how much Maya was paid by the Morellis— or by my ex-wife's lawyers, Connor Truman and Veronica Fischer, who were also conspiring against me. Maya started to buttonhole my other employees—nurses, techs, and even the other doctor, Jimmy Black—and persuade them to turn against me.

My ex-wife's goal was to destroy me at any cost, to have my medical license revoked and ruin my professional and personal reputation. Before my father died, he had offered her a million dollars to stay out of my life and the lives of all our family members, but she had refused the offer. "I want the money from Dino," she had said, "or else I will do everything

possible to destroy his professional career and put him in jail."
And that's exactly what was going on as she conspired with
the Morellis.

The behavior of Jimmy Black, the doctor, surprised me.
He was incompetent and made many mistakes, so I was going
to get rid of him eventually. But when I found out that he was
part of the collusion, I fired him on the spot. He flew into a
fury, ranting and raving in the middle of the office. He had
applied for privileges at the local hospital in Arizona, where
I was chairman of surgery, but I wouldn't allow him in the
operating room because of his incompetence. He couldn't
make it in Las Vegas, where he lived because of his professional
incompetence and inability to get along with other people.

After that, my nurse practitioner left and took three of my
techs with her. My medical office manager, Marian Klein,
was still with me, but she was as spooked as anyone else.
She too had received threatening phone calls at home. She
wouldn't reveal the details to me, but she said she couldn't
stand the pressure and was going to resign.

I tried to get her to stay. "Please, I just need proper ancillary
support. I need you. You can't leave me in the middle of a
crisis. My whole practice is falling apart because of lack of
personnel!" But I couldn't persuade her to stay, so she quit too.

I was in a real predicament. Patients were calling, operations
needed to be scheduled, and I didn't have the staff to handle
things. I was able to bring somebody in part-time, but they

were not equipped to handle the workload. It finally got to the point where patients were at risk because I was unable to provide medical care. So with great emotional distress, I closed my practice for reasons of patient safety.

I tried to re-staff. Sofia invested in the practice and allowed me to lease equipment from her firm to keep the office open. Before it was all over, she had poured $400,000 into the business (which was later paid back) and come to work in the office herself, but it was an unsustainable situation. No one wanted to work for me, because they knew the Morellis were after me and threatening anyone who joined my team.

It was clear that the Morellis had conspired with Veronica Fischer and Connor Truman, my ex-wife's lawyers, as well as news organizations in Indiana and Bartholomew County.

My ex-wife, Chelsea, whom I met when I was in the final year of my residency in 1987, had been a beautiful woman. Five foot ten in height, she had long brown hair and a thin, athletic build. She was uneducated but street smart and cunning, and she used her looks to get what she wanted. Chelsea didn't know how to cook, so she tended to eat at McDonald's and other fast-food restaurants. Her bad nutritional habits did not help her aging process in any way, and during our marriage she aged rather quickly. I learned later in our marriage that Chelsea was devious and untrustworthy, an addict, a pathological liar, and dangerous.

During the divorce, she hired Veronica Fischer, an attorney who was ugly and obese and had short fire-red hair. Fischer, who spoke in an angry voice, was arrogant and corrupt. She paid the AP wire service to destroy my professional reputation through the dissemination of false information and submitted to the *20/20* news program a fraudulent report that claimed that I had conspired to murder my ex-wife. When this fraudulent misinformation was described to a friend of mine in Hollywood, he warned *20/20* that broadcasting it would result in a treacherous legal battle, which they would lose. After subsequently contacting me through an intermediary, *20/20* dismissed the report that Veronica Fischer had submitted to them.

Eventually I met with the hospital administration, who claimed that they wanted to employ me to shield me from the Morellis, who were creating patient safety issues for my practice.

I told them, "There is no way I can continue fighting these false accusations alone while I am trying to conduct a large solo medical practice. You have to help me out here, because otherwise I'll have to leave over these patient safety issues."

I had a lot of expensive medical and surgical equipment that they were to buy, along with my office equipment, as part of the proposed employment agreement. But they made me a ridiculously low offer that didn't cover a fraction of the cost of the medical equipment, so I turned them down.

I said, "Listen, fix this issue. I'm taking a sabbatical, effective immediately. Unless and until you fix this issue, I will be unable to operate here or have my patients cared for here in a safe fashion."

As if that wasn't enough, Margaret Morelli, working for Truman and Fischer, began to claim, fraudulently and publicly, that there was a warrant out for my arrest because I had failed to pay child support—which was obviously not true. She took the fraudulent, doctored document from Fischer and sent it to all the local physicians who have referred patients to me. They were attempting to starve me out.

One night it all came to a head when my life itself was threatened. I was working late, long after midnight, and a man I believed to be a patient came into my office.

I sat with him and asked, "How can I help?"

He pulled a handgun from his belt and put it on my desk. I had been in threatening situations before, but I was instantly nervous since we were the only two people in the office.

He said, "You know, Doc, your other patients have nothing but good things to say about you. I've talked to some of them, sitting out there in the waiting room, and they have only high praise for you."

Trying to keep the conversation civil, I said, "Thank you. I try to do my best."

Then he said, "Some people in town don't like you and don't want you here. They want to see you severely penalized. I'm just the messenger, here to tell you to stop doing what you're doing." Then he stood, picked up his gun, and left.

I reported the incident to the police, too, of course, but they couldn't do anything. The man had provided no identification, he'd booked the appointment under a false name, and when they dusted the chair that he had put his hands on, there were no fingerprints.

I felt like I could have been murdered at any moment after that. Clearly Dr. Morelli was a psychopath. I knew he kept a whole arsenal of guns, from automatic weapons to shotguns, and he was a trained marksman. So I went out and bought weapons of my own, to defend myself if need be, and I hired a security guard to follow me around. I had guns at my bedside, in my office, and in my car. Even my cane, the result of a spinal injury from 2009, was a weapon.

CHAPTER THREE

Attempted Murder

I was unconscious on my bedroom floor, trapped under boxes, having suffered traumatic injuries to my legs and right hip and at risk of death from renal failure. My phone's battery was already dead; it lay useless beside me.

Miss Lombardi had no way of knowing that, however, so after several failed attempts to reach me, she decided to try Nassif, who was totally unaware of the conflicts that I had with him and my concerns going forward. She was able to persuade him to drive to my house and see if I was there.

Nassif was on the phone with her when he arrived at my front door, but of course his knocking drew no response. Then she asked him to walk around the house and knock on the patio door that led directly into the master bedroom. He followed her instructions and pounded on the glass door, calling my name all the while.

Somehow, almost miraculously, I regained enough consciousness to register the pounding and shouting. My cane had fallen beside me, but it was not trapped by the boxes like I was. Fortunately it was within reach, and using all my strength, I managed to use it to unlock the door latch, allowing Nassif to enter the room.

Sofia was still instructing him by phone. When he told her the condition in which he'd found me, she knew I must be overdue for my weekly injection. As a type two diabetic, I was taking Byetta weekly injections, metformin in pill form, and occasional insulin injections. Even when someone with diabetes pays close attention to their diet, exercises regularly, and takes their prescribed medication, external conditions such as stress can cause a blood sugar spike.

Nassif walked into my kitchen and looked in my refrigerator to find the Byetta injection pen. He brought it back with him, but then made the absurd claim that he didn't know how to administer the injection. So he gave the pen to me and I injected myself, which I'd done so many times that I could manage it even in my feeble condition.

Miss Lombardi told Nassif that I needed something to eat to regain my strength, and astonishingly, rather than go into our kitchen, he left the house! When he returned, he was no longer on the phone; she had left me in what she assumed were good hands. Nassif gave me a chicken sandwich and a bottle of Gatorade, which contained high fructose corn syrup and high levels of potassium, which would accentuate kidney issues by spiking my potassium levels. Did he not know anything about diabetes or renal failure, or was he just being a sadist by offering me something that could have killed me? Was it intentional? It didn't matter. I had already been pinned under the boxes for days without food or drink, so I would have taken anything.

I ate and drank, but I was still immobilized on the floor. I pleaded to Nassif to help me get free. "Please, please, get me free from these boxes so that I can get up. I'm in so much pain. You need to get these boxes off my legs so that I can get out of this contorted position. Please help me!"

I needed to get up! Even if I wasn't able to make it to a doctor to have my injured legs treated, I could at least rest in bed until I felt a little better. It would have been obvious to anyone that I was in great pain and distress, but thanks to his medical training, Dr. Nassif should have also noticed other things—like my confused, incoherent speech—and realized that something else was going on.

Because of my leg injuries and encroaching kidney failure, the toxins in my bloodstream were beginning to cause delirium and cognitive impairment. Again and again, I asked Nassif, who worked out in the gym every day and was rather strong, to lift the boxes off my legs. Finally, he squatted beside me and made a feeble attempt to move one box. He made a face as though he was straining with all his might, but even in my injured state, I could see that he was acting. He planned to leave me pinned in place, unable to escape or interfere with whatever he had in mind. Rage raced through my mind.

I began to wonder what he was going to do. Drop another box on my head and kill me? Fear rushed through my veins. I couldn't let him know of my suspicions, though, so I tried to keep him talking to me.

I asked him to plug in my phone and place it within reach, but he ignored me. Then I asked him to call 911 so they could free me, since he couldn't, but he made no response to that request either. Can you imagine a doctor looking at someone who had been grievously injured and not only failing to help them, but refusing to reach out for assistance? My legs were swollen to three times their normal size. I was in crisis, and this man—whom I considered, if not a friend, at least a trusted business partner—was doing nothing! This was basically the equivalent of murder.

Then Nassif went one step further, from what a lawyer might call "depraved indifference" to outright hostile action. With one more glance at me lying in agony on the floor, he walked out of the bedroom and into the dining room. I could barely make out his conversation, but he was calling his lawyer. He stayed in the dining room for an outrageous length of time, getting advice on how to deal with me. Finally he reappeared in the bedroom doorway.

With a cocky smirk on his face, he sat down beside me, perched on a box. In a small act of mercy, he did not sit on one of the boxes crushing my limbs. With a gleam in his eye, he looked down at me on the floor and asked, "Do you want me to call an ambulance?"

I responded, "Of course I do!" I could see his phone still in his hand, so I suspected that he was recording our conversation and wondered why he would do such a thing. But my brain was fogged with toxins, and I could not concentrate enough to reason my way through the situation. I was reduced to responding only to the most important things.

"Yes," I groaned. Of course I wanted him to call an ambulance! It must have been obvious to him that in addition to my leg injuries, I was suffering renal failure. I was drifting in and out of consciousness, nearly comatose.

Then I looked him straight in the eye, with all the energy that remained in my injured, weakened body, and repeated my request for assistance. It occurred to me, as I lay there, that I could feel my organs shutting down. I had not urinated or defecated for several days, and the level of toxins in my body was exhausting me. I was convinced that without rescue, I was going to die right there on my bedroom floor. I was worth more to Nassif dead than alive, considering that I would obviously need extended hospitalization. So it was easier for him to let me die than to save me and go to the expense of paying me.

Perhaps I should explain exactly what was going on with my body, so that you can understand my physical and psychological status at the time. When you suffer a crushing injury to the muscles of any limb, damaged skeletal muscle tissue breaks down rapidly. This condition, called rhabdomyolysis, causes toxins to leach into the bloodstream, travel to the kidneys, and plug them up, impeding their function. Some of these toxins, such as the protein myoglobin, are extremely harmful to the kidneys and will lead to kidney failure, which ultimately leads to multiple system organ failure. Thus I was in grave danger, which got worse the longer I went without medical care.

Nassif looked at me and nodded. He assured me that he would call an ambulance to help me, and then he walked out of the room, closing the patio door behind him. He was gone, and I was alone.

I lay on the floor for hours waiting for someone to come and save me. I was delirious and flickering on the edge of unconsciousness, but in my moments of lucidity I reminded myself that Dr. Nassif was a doctor. He had taken the same Hippocratic Oath that I had, the one that began with the words, "First, do no harm." Surely he must have known that by leaving me alone, injured and helpless, he was doing harm, but why? Obviously it came down to money. He had chosen to murder me for financial gain. The sun rose and set again and again, but no ambulance came.

I had been living in Rome, Italy, in 2014 when Dr. Nassif reached out and invited me to come to the United States to set up a new division of his practice to treat patients in need of urological care. I had no interest in returning to the United States at that time; he had sought me out.

Another urological group, Urology Health Group, already had an established presence in the area, including a relationship with the administrators at the local hospital. This group had battled with Nassif, even boycotting his radiation therapy treatments to patients, but Nassif didn't warn me about the deep ties between those doctors and the local hospitals. He had made a casual reference to bad blood, but the fact was that the urology group had refused to care for any of Nassif's patients suffering complications related to radiation therapy of prostate cancers. That's what had inspired Nassif to get his own urologist—me.

Should I have realized that the urology group would react poorly to an outsider coming in and potentially harming the profitable business they had going, headed by Luis Perez, MD? Perhaps. But Nassif had hidden the truth from me. He wanted someone with a strong background and the leadership ability to set up a competitive urology division and care for patients in need of urological attention, and I was an ideal candidate. I brought vast experience and innovative surgical techniques, and it seemed that Nassif recognized my value, because he had offered to pay me handsomely.

As everyone knows, Florida has a large population of senior citizens and retirees. Many of these people suffer from urological problems, including prostate and bladder cancers. Thus it was an ideal place for Nassif to set up a practice offering radiation treatment—and to bring me in to handle the surgical side, even though he was being blackballed by the urology group in town. It was my understanding that the local hospitals were equipped to handle the type of work that I needed to do, to provide proper patient care. It all looked good.

So in January of 2014 I left Rome, where I had been setting up a practice and considering establishing a new urology division at the University of Rome, and returned to the United States, accepting what initially seemed like a handsome offer worthy of my skills and experience.

However, I quickly learned that things were not as they seemed. Nassif had painted a wildly inaccurate picture of the actual market conditions, and his practice was actually suffering. The competing urology practice was also doing radiation therapy of the prostate, competing directly with Dr. Nassif's practice and eating into his profits. When I saw the numbers, it was obvious that the area could not support a second urological practice. Disillusioned, I contacted recruiters and quickly began to look for other positions. In fact I had another interview in Clearwater, Florida, scheduled for two days after my accident, but obviously I was not able to get to it. Nassif was in over his head, but we had a financial agreement, so there was little he could do in the interim.

Our relationship became challenging. I had been doing surgical hydrocele repairs in the office and other surgeries in the outpatient facility under local anesthesia while waiting for my hospital privileges to come through.

Nassif told me, "You're doing good work, Dino. But you still need to send me more patients for radiation therapy for their prostate cancer."

I was doing good work, treating patients and making a name for myself in the area, but as I explained earlier, my preferred surgical options did not generate as much profit as radiation treatments. Also, I stood my ground on maintaining my ethics and standards of care. Furthermore, Nassif was required to pay me for the use of my equipment, which quickly became an expense he couldn't handle.

My accident was a stroke of luck for Nassif. If I died, all expenses associated with my department would die with me. He would no longer have to pay my salary or equipment rental fees, on which he was already months behind, and he would be free to run his struggling practice any way he saw fit. This, I believe, was the substance of the conversation he had with his lawyer while I lay in agony on the floor. He was deciding how he could let me die without being culpable. The two of them ultimately agreed that he should just walk away, leaving me helpless and alone. I see no way to describe these actions other than as conspiracy to commit murder.

But the universe had other plans.

CHAPTER FOUR

My Death

My accident happened the week before Memorial Day weekend. It wasn't until Tuesday morning, when I failed to arrive at the office at eight o'clock, that my staff began to wonder whether something was wrong.

Two of my most trusted and loyal employees were my office manager, Maria, and my nurse, Courtney. Maria, attractive with short blond hair, was married with children. A dedicated office manager who never gave up, she always found a solution to the problems associated with setting up my practice. Courtney, also attractive at five foot six with brown hair, had a gift for interpersonal relationships with patients. My patients loved both Maria and Courtney.

I had hired each of them, giving them their first jobs in urological medicine, and Nassif had little control over them. I was training them, because I have always believed that mentorship, building relationships based on trust, and providing opportunities are crucial elements of the bond between a doctor and his staff. The people who work in your office are not your servants; they are members of a team whose job is to help you do your best and provide your patients with the best possible care.

Before I was scheduled to do a physical examination, they would've already entered the patient's intake, vital signs, urine analysis, medical history, and all other pertinent information into the electronic medical record. This was time-consuming work, so I delegated it to my staff in order to increase my efficiency. This also gave my staff a sense of fulfillment in direct patient care.

I treat my staff well, educating them along the way. Staff members must be trustworthy, but they must also see that you rely on them to be every bit as committed to the success of the office and the patients' treatment as you are. This was my relationship with Maria and Courtney.

However, Maria and Courtney were afraid of Dr. Nassif, who was a powerful figure in the local medical Muslim community. A lot of Muslim doctors in the community supported him, and as newcomers to the field, Maria and Courtney didn't want to run afoul of him and damage their future career prospects.

Nassif was a hypocritical, fake Muslim, because he drank alcohol, ate pork, and did not conform to the ideals of his faith. He constantly ridiculed his Muslim colleagues for their social interactions with the community.

One day I said to him, "So you drink wine and liquor, eat pork, don't pray, and don't conform to the religious beliefs of your Muslim colleagues. Why do you call yourself a Muslim?"

He answered, "It's for political and business reasons. You see, Muslims will tend to refer to a Muslim physician, so it's a way of self-preservation for me and my practice."

When he called my team into his office on May 26, 2015, right after my accident, as I learned later, they were uncertain about what he could possibly want from them. It turned out that he wanted them to sign papers asserting that they would not provide me with any sort of assistance, without being told what this referred to. Furthermore, the papers included a confidentiality agreement, which meant that when they became aware of my situation, they couldn't tell anyone what was going on.

Still, I wasn't around and they were concerned. As decent human beings, they felt the need to get to the bottom of what was going on. They called me repeatedly, but they got no answer since my phone was dead. It wasn't like me not to answer my phone, so after several hours of trying, they decided to drive to my house and check on me. They knew that I had checked out of my hotel in New Orleans over a week earlier, but had I actually returned home from the American Urological

Association conference? They knew that I was alone, and perhaps I was sick.

As trusted employees, they had been to my house many times and had the code to my front gate. They let themselves onto the property, rang the bell, and then tried the door, which Nassif must have left unlocked. Inside the house, they called my name, but I was unconscious on the bedroom floor, crushed and in agony.

As mentioned earlier, I am reconstructing these events from fragments of memory and information given to me by other people after the fact. As my neurologist explained to me, toxins from renal failure build up in the brain and affect the limbic system and hippocampus, which controls memory. Once these toxins have been present long enough, they can temporarily or permanently destroy brain cells and memories.

As I lay there helpless, watching the sun rise and set in my stuporous state, with brief periods of awareness, something miraculous happened! It was the most blissful experience I've ever had. I was overcome by joy, reawakened to alertness, and instantly aware of every aspect of my surroundings. I was no longer in pain, and I felt like I was weightless and free to move without any restrictions. What was going on?

It was as though I was hovering near the ceiling fan, and I looked down and saw a man buried under a pile of boxes on the floor. As I looked closer, I realized that the man was me. I wondered, *Am I dead? Did I die? Is this what death is about?*

I was still able to see my arms and legs, but I felt no pain. I was like a spirit, able to fly, and a sense of weightlessness and sheer splendor had overcome my entire being.

The moment that I realized that I was outside my body and gazing down upon myself, I was drawn into a magnificent world that appeared like clouds surrounding me on all sides. I had no direct ability to maneuver myself, but I was being pulled upward into a beautiful, serene, bright, opaque tunnel of clouds. I could feel a breeze blowing against my face, and I had a sense of joy and peace without a care in the world.

The sides of the tunnel were lined with faces and scenes from my life. I was transported upward, for what felt like half an hour, in the most blissful experience that I've ever surrendered to. Finally, I stopped at a place where the clouds seemed to end. They were like puffs of smoke moving outward from the center of the tunnel, as if a geyser was puffing them toward the walls.

Still hovering in a weightless state, I then heard a masculine voice speaking in a language that I did not recognize. It was a kind, warm, fatherly voice that brought me perfect tranquility. I listened attentively, trying to make out what he was saying, but it was as if I did not have to understand it. Instead, I felt it! The words instilled a sense of calmness in me, and I was not afraid at all.

As the voice spoke, the clouds would move with each word. I was in awe, unable to express what I was feeling. As I listened, I heard other voices whispering in the background. I stared at the white glowing wall of clouds, and a sense of meaning was bestowed upon me. My soul was able to decipher the words, leaving me in the most peaceful state that I've ever experienced. It was a period of timelessness and ecstasy, and I did not want it to end.

I don't know how much time passed while this message was being given to me, but it transformed me in a way that can't be described by words alone. I was enchanted, like a moth hovering around a light bulb, receiving a message that I did not understand.

Suddenly I was transported back down the tunnel to Earth, where I felt agonizing pain. My body convulsed as surges of electricity passed through me. I believe this was when I died and went into asystole, better known as cardiac arrest. The EMTs had to cardiovert me and restore my heart from arrhythmia to a normal rhythm using electricity. At this time I must explain that when one is in renal failure, the kidneys cannot excrete potassium. When too much potassium builds up in the blood, it will stop the heart from beating, a form of cardiac arrest called asystole. To restart the heart, a procedure called cardioversion can be used, which consists of administering electrical currents to the heart along with potassium-lowering drugs.

It's amazing to me that I remember everything about that experience but little that happened before or afterward. Apparently I had a near-death experience, and it changed my life completely. I remember it vividly and often wish I had never left that blissful state and returned to Earth, but God gave me a message that day.

I believe the male voice was probably Jesus Christ telling me that I had more things to accomplish in my life to help others. Was it meant for me to continue practicing medicine and helping patients? Or was I meant to write these words so that if you, the reader, have any question about the existence of Jesus Christ or God, you'll never doubt it again? As I write this, I still get goose bumps reliving that experience in my mind. Reader, wake up! There is a God, a Jesus Christ, and a heaven, and I can't wait to return there to experience more of the magnificence that God has to offer us. May God bless us all!

I am told that when Maria and Courtney entered the bedroom and saw me on the floor beside my dead cell phone and cane, with boxes crushing my legs, they cried out in shock. One of them immediately pulled her cell phone from her purse and called for an ambulance, while the other shifted the boxes—with ease, I am told—to free my swollen, grievously injured legs. They waited with me, knowing to leave me undisturbed, until the EMTs arrived about fifteen minutes later. By that time, I was in a coma and so far gone with renal failure that I went into cardiac arrest from the elevated potassium levels in my blood. The EMTs had to defibrillate me and restart my heart twice in the ambulance en route to the hospital.

When Sofia called either Maria or Courtney and learned that I was in the hospital, she was shocked. She had sent Nassif to the house to check on me, and she didn't understand why he hadn't called an ambulance upon finding me in such dire condition. There must have been some kind of miscommunication, she assumed. However, I believe that if someone checked Nassif's phone records and triangulated his location, they'd find that his only call that afternoon had been to his lawyer, Kenneth Weise.

My memory of what happened next is completely gone, apparently from the toxins seeping into my brain. But I can say this without fear of contradiction: if Maria and Courtney had not come to my rescue, I would be dead, just as Nassif had planned.

The EMTs transported me to the hospital, and the doctors later told me that had I not received medical attention within hours, I would have died. In fact, when I first arrived at the hospital, they didn't expect me to survive. They did scans of my legs and brain, and a battery of blood tests confirmed that I was in a coma from acute renal failure.

In addition to the multiple organ system failure, something else was going on with my heart, so they performed a transesophageal echocardiography on me. To do this procedure, they inserted a probe into my mouth, down my throat, and into my esophagus to take ultrasound pictures of my heart. This revealed cardiac vegetation—bacterial growth—on one of the valves of my heart, a condition known as endocarditis. This told them that a blood-borne pathogen or bacteria was inducing my high fever. This was probably as a result of one of the punctures through my skin, on my right leg from the dirty boxes inoculating an infection, which became blood-borne and seeded the cardiac valves.

After consulting a cardiac surgeon, the team determined that I needed a cardiac valve replacement immediately. But when a cardiologist/internal medicine/infectious disease specialist—probably one of the best doctors on the team— was consulted and reviewed the ultrasound films of my heart, he thought that antibiotic therapy might be a better choice. So there was a conflict.

Cardiac surgeons were born to cut people open, and it's a piece of cake for them to do a cardiac valve replacement. But there are significant side effects, especially when the patient has acute renal failure and is undergoing dialysis, as I was. The potential for excessive bleeding is high.

To deliver medications and allow me to undergo dialysis, the doctors placed a central venous catheter, which is a large tube, into the subclavian vein that runs up the right arm from just above the clavicle and near the heart. The records indicate that I had dialysis immediately, but when toxins in the bloodstream reach a certain level, they must be removed slowly to prevent the patient from going into shock. There is also the possibility of herniation of the brain stem, which can turn the patient into a vegetable because of fluid shifts that occur during the process. They had to perform slow dialysis on me twice a day for a month, and I was comatose for most of that time, which created even greater risks.

When I look at the medical bills, I am astonished by how many doctors had to work together to keep me alive. From nephrology for my kidneys, to neurology for my brain, to cardiology and cardiac surgery for my heart, to infectious disease and internal medicine specialists … I must have presented quite a challenge, and I'm grateful to every one of them.

When Sofia found out that I was in the hospital, she immediately began the journey back to Florida to see me. She was out on bail, paid with her own money, and her bail bondsman said she was free to go anywhere she wanted as long as she returned to court on June 5. However, she had no money, credit cards, or identification. How was she supposed to get from Indiana to Florida, when she couldn't rent a car or take a bus or plane? The police certainly weren't about to help her.

Sofia and Dick, her son, made it out of Noblesville, Indiana, by just walking down the road. Two women and a teenage boy stopped and gave them a ride nearly to the Indiana state line. They kept traveling that way, relying on help from strangers on their journey from Indiana to Florida. When they were within fifty miles of Resort City Beach, Sofia called Courtney and Maria, who picked her up and took her right to my room in the hospital's intensive care unit.

When I saw her, we talked just like we always had in the past, but I have no memory of that. She visited me every day, but we'd always talk about the same things because I could never remember what we had talked about on the previous day. I couldn't remember Sofia's arrest or what had happened during those lost days in my bedroom. As far as my brain was concerned, I had never gone to the urological convention in New Orleans. Months of my life were gone and have never returned.

When I was released from the hospital, I talked to many people, trying to piece together that period of my life. The more I heard, the more horrified I was about Dr. Nassif's treatment of me. I asked Maria and Courtney what had gone on in the office in my absence, so that I could file a police report. I needed their help and support to show what a depraved individual Dr. Nassif was. In fact, I wanted him charged with attempted murder for leaving me in my bedroom to die.

Beatrice, one of my first assistant nurses, told me that when this incident occurred, Dr. Nassif had called Maria, Courtney, and Rosie (the receptionist) into his office. He had them sign confidentiality agreements indicating that they were not to help me, communicate with me, or talk about this matter with anyone. These issues terrified and confused Rosie, Maria, and Courtney. In fact, when I was going to file the police report against Nassif, Maria and Courtney told Beatrice that they could not come forward because of the agreement that they had signed. However, Rosie, a person of great integrity, was not afraid of either the truth or Dr. Nassif. In fact, she had stayed at my bedside for many days to keep me company.

In November 2015, Beatrice provided me with a sworn, notarized affidavit including the details of the attempted murder by Nassif and how he tried to use the confidentiality and nondisclosure agreement to prevent the truth from coming out. Since there is no statute of limitations for attempted murder, this leaves an open avenue for the future. I will be forever grateful to all of my medical assistants for what they did for me.

Here is the text of Beatrice's sworn affidavit:

Sworn affidavit by Beatrice Newman-Ballinger, RN, LMT

November 23, 2015

Re: Dr. Dino Panvini (confidential & protected); Dr. Abdul Nassif; Kenneth Weise, AAL; Courtney Addington, and Maria Ewing Duff.

On August 8, 2015, I spoke face-to-face with Maria Duff, LPN, with whom I previously worked at the Urology Center, along with Courtney Addington, Office Manager, and Dr. Dino Panvini. I, unfortunately, had to resign my position as RN on May 8, 2015, due to a near-fatal automobile accident involving my father, in Alabama, that occurred on Thursday, April 30, 2015. I returned from Alabama on June 8, 2015.

Maria Duff, LPN, on August 8, 2015, relayed a near-fatal event regarding Dr. Dino Panvini. She told me that Dr. Panvini left the Urology Center, after all patients were seen, on Tuesday, May 11, 2015, to prepare for departure on Wednesday, May 12, 2015, to attend the American Urological Association Conference in New Orleans. He was expected to return to Florida on Tuesday, May 19, 2015, and to his office on Tuesday, May 26, 2015. However, Dr. Panvini made no contact with the office on May 26, 2015, to notify anyone that he would need to be out and to have his patients' appointments rescheduled. Courtney and Maria tried to reach him by cellphone and home phone, to no avail.

According to Maria Duff, LPN, she and Courtney, Office Manager, contacted Dr. Nassif (of the Cancer Center, Resort City Beach, Florida), Dr. Panvini's business partner, on Wednesday, May 20, 2015, regarding Dr. Panvini's absence. However, Dr. Nassif did not go over to check on his partner until three full days later, on Friday, May 22, 2015, finding him in a debilitated state with boxes of books on his body.

After having this face-to-face meeting with Maria Duff, LPN, on August 8, 2015, I immediately called Courtney Addington, Office Manager, to discuss the events that occurred from Wednesday, May 19, 2015, to Tuesday, May 26, 2015. Courtney told the exact same description of the atrocities that were committed by Dr. Nassif on Friday, May 22, 2015.

This is the "rest of the story!" Maria had told me that Dr. Panvini had been admitted to HPMC Resort City Beach on Tuesday May, 26, 2015, after Courtney and Maria went over to his home to check on him, finding him in the same crumpled position, with all the boxes of books still on his body, from his collapse on Wednesday, May 19, 2015. They immediately called 911 and Dr. Panvini lifted his eyes and arms to say, "Thank you for saving my life," as he passed out. When Dr. Panvini was put in the ambulance, his heart stopped and the EMTs had to defibrillate him twice. Dr. Panvini was admitted directly to ICU at HPMC, entering into renal failure and coma. The doctors and nurses told Maria and Courtney that he would have not survived if they had been even one minute later in obtaining emergency care for him. Maria told me that he stayed at HPMC for two months before being transferred to Health North.

On August 8, 2015, after hearing all of the atrocities committed by Dr. Abdul Nassif and being told by Maria that Dr. Panvini was presently in rehabilitation at Health North, I went over to Health North but the front-desk receptionist said that he had been recently discharged. I called Maria to get Dr. Panvini's cellphone number. I left him a message in reference to all that I was just informed of by Maria and Courtney and to let him know that I had tried to go see him at Health North.

Let it be known that Dr. Nassif called in Courtney and Maria after their rescue of Dr. Panvini on Tuesday, May 26, 2015, and demanded their keys to Dr. Dino Panvini's office, thereby terminating them without warning or reason. Dr. Nassif went even further to demand, in writing, that they were to have "no contact with Dr. Panvini!" Maria said that Dr. Nassif said that if they had contact with Dr. Dino Panvini, they would be put on a "black ball" list, thereby preventing them from being employed by another potential employer.

I had another contact with Dr. Panvini via cellphone on October 22, 2015, to discuss the atrocities committed by Dr. Nassif. In a detailed account of events as described by Courtney, Maria, and even Dr. Panvini, Dr. Nassif maliciously intended to cause deadly harm to Dr. Panvini! Dr. Abdul Nassif used the business credit card on Thursday, May 22, 2015, to buy a Subway sandwich for Dr. Panvini. Before Dr. Nassif even touched Dr. Panvini, he made a call to his lawyer, Kenneth Weise, for legal advice. Even in his debilitated state, Dr. Panvini overheard the conversation that Dr. Nassif had with Kenneth Weise, Esq. Dr. Panvini was found in a crumpled, crippled state on the floor of his bedroom at his home, under boxes of books and diplomas that he was trying to move from one place to another, as he passed out on Tuesday, May 19, 2015. Dr. Panvini attested to the fact that Dr. Abdul Nassif, finding him in this debilitated state, proceeded to give Dr. Panvini medication and put the Subway sandwich beside his body. Dr. Panvini stated that Dr. Nassif left him in this condition and left his home at 2020 Harbor Drive, Resort City Beach, Florida, and never even called 911 or returned.

Based on these facts, I, Beatrice Newman-Ballinger, RN, LMT, do hereby serve this Sworn

Affidavit as "witness" to attempted homicide of Dr. Dino Panvini by Dr. Abdul Nassif. The accomplice to this crime would be Dr. Nassif's lawyer, Kenneth Weise, Attorney at Law. I expect Justice to be served!

Respectfully submitted,

Beatrice Newman-Ballinger, RN, LMT

P.S. My contact information is …

The county police were so corrupt that they would do anything to protect Nassif, because he was a prominent doctor in the community. Because of my frail physical condition, I was limited to a walker and unable to drive. So I contacted the sheriff's office to have one of the police officers come to my house to take an official report for attempted murder by Dr. Nassif. However, the police adamantly refused to do so because they knew of him.

Beatrice told me later that the police protect their own doctors, whatever the facts may be. This is very disturbing, since police are supposed to uphold the law. They are required to take reports on criminal behavior, but they refused to take any report from me! This shows you the level of police corruption in Resort City Beach, Florida.

CHAPTER FIVE

The Theft

I spent many months recuperating in medical centers in Resort City Beach. I underwent dialysis, multiple surgeries and procedures, and recuperative physical therapy, all while maintaining the treatment regimen for my diabetes. I had suffered extensive physical and mental damage; my legs had been crushed, and the muscles took a long time to recover. I had been walking with a cane even before the accident, and now it was even worse. When I left the hospital, I was using a walker.

Furthermore, after my accident I was desperately afraid of falling and having no way to contact the outside world. I carried my cell phone in a pouch I had made and attached to a string around my neck so that it would always be with me— just in case I fell and couldn't get up. I even contemplated getting a First Alert medical signaling device, but I felt that the cell phone was a better solution.

The mental costs of my ordeal were possibly even more awful than the physical ones. I still had perfect use of my hands, so once I got back on my feet with my internal organs functioning properly, I could've returned to practicing medicine, even performing operations on patients. But my mind was not what it had been, and there were large gaps in my memory.

I'm convinced that if Connor Truman and Veronica Fischer had not conspired with the Morellis and my ex-wife, I would never have left Arizona and none of this would've happened. I would still have been practicing in Arizona if my ex-wife and her co-conspirators had not maliciously invaded my life to destroy me.

I couldn't remember attending the urological conference in New Orleans—an entire week of my life, gone. The days I had spent trapped in my bedroom existed only as short flashes of memory, creating periods of severe anxiety. I remembered the boxes falling on me. I remembered Nassif looking down at me as I lay there in agony; talking to his lawyer Kenneth Weise instead of calling for help; offering me food and drink that was worse for me than if I'd eaten nothing at all; and finally sitting beside me with a sardonic grin, asking if I wanted him to call an ambulance, all the while knowing he was going to do nothing. And I remembered Maria and Courtney, my true saviors, finding me and summoning help at last, literally saving my life when I was on the brink of death.

In the hospital, I had continued to slip in and out of awareness. I had been unconscious for a long time while my system was flushed out with dialysis, my heart was repaired with antibiotics, and my organs slowly returned to normal function. But even when I was awake, life was a blur. I had almost no memory of my hospital stay until recently, though now my memory of that time has almost completely returned.

For example, I was apparently visited several times by my friend Sofia Lombardi. And though her mother, Helen, assured me that Sofia and I spent many hours together while I recovered from my injuries and ailments, I have no memory of even a single conversation between us.

Furthermore, there are no photographs, social media posts, or anything else to indicate that Sofia was ever in my hospital room. The only way I know for sure that she—and more particularly, *Dick*—came to Florida after my accident was that my house was robbed while I was hospitalized.

Dick, Sofia's son, was thin and sickly looking because of his chronic drug abuse and addiction to heroin. Rather short for his age, Dick had an angry demeanor—as most thieves do. When I came home from the hospital, I discovered to my horror that Dick had ransacked my house. All my money was gone, along with the Glock pistol I'd purchased for protection while living out west, bottles of prescription drugs, a collection of gold coins, and many other valuables.

It was a lucky break for Dick that I had only recently returned to the United States from Italy, and that because of the fraught situation between my ex-wife and me, I had been reluctant to put all of my money in the bank. There had been about $250,000 in cash in the house, along with another $100,000 or so in gold coins—American Eagles, buffalo coins, liberty coins, and Krugerrands. Some had been given to me by my father, and others I had collected as an investment vehicle. I kept them in an album for archival purposes and stored them in one of three safes in the house, all of which were opened and emptied.

Dick was a professional thief who had been arrested previously on other cases of larceny and drug possession. I can say with 100 percent certainty that it was Dick who robbed me—and more or less wiped me out in the process—because of evidence directly linking him to the crime. His mother confirmed that he then went to San Diego, where he left the money with his father and sold the coins in a pawnshop. I am amazed at the obvious corruption of this malignant, parasitic drug addict and criminal, to take advantage of somebody on the brink of death. He, too, probably expected me to die. But God had other plans.

I was new to Resort City Beach, with no friends in town except my coworkers. Dick was one of the few people who had known that I had items of value in my house and that I would be away for an extended period of time. Helen told me that Dick was the only person who had been at my house alone without my knowledge. My gut feeling is that he went to the house and wiped out my cash reserves and valuables as part of a plan to get himself out of the country and escape punishment for the crimes for which he and Sofia had been arrested in Indiana.

I had never liked Dick Lombardi. The entire time I knew him, which was only because of the stress and problems he caused his mother while we were together, he was a drug addict and a criminal. Sofia told me that Dick used heroin and other intravenous and smokable narcotics, and that he had been convicted of theft and drug possession multiple times. She had lost all control of her son, who had been in and out of jail since he was young, creating havoc with his mother's life. Dick was a true hoodlum.

Still, Sofia was fiercely loyal to her son, and she never seemed to lose faith that he would one day live up to his potential. I will say that despite his addictions, he was an extremely intelligent young man, capable of working miracles with computers and technology. Ironically, it was perhaps this ability that allowed him to open three different safes in my house, without knowing any of the combinations.

Both Sofia and Dick had to be back in Indiana by June 5 to appear in court, but they had no money or means of supporting themselves. Taking the money from my house would provide Dick with the means to escape, if that was what he chose to do … which, as it turned out, is exactly what he had in mind.

CHAPTER SIX

Legal Corruption

What I have to say now is based entirely on information from other sources—newspaper articles, TV news, the internet, court transcripts, personal interrogation transcripts, and testimony from other people. It all happened while I was in the hospital recovering from my accident, and I was not involved with it in any way.

Because I was incapacitated, even comatose for several months, I did not know why Sofia and her junkie son, Dick, had been arrested in Indiana. It didn't even occur to me to wonder what they were doing there. We actually broke up before any of this took place—the accident, her arrest, any of it. I had not seen her for perhaps a month beforehand.

In our final conversation before my accident, she had told me that she was going to visit Dick. He was living in San Diego, California, where his father lives, but I believe that Sofia was going to meet him somewhere on the East Coast. I wasn't concerned about it, to be honest. I was headed to New Orleans, and I had my own life to worry about. And when Sofia called me to bail her out of jail, I was too incoherent to give it much thought. I responded almost by reflex, handling the situation as quickly as possible with her own funds.

It wasn't until after I had recovered from my accident and all the resulting surgeries and medical interventions that it began to sink in for me. While I had been convalescing, fading in and out of consciousness, Sofia had been in town to visit me. It was during that time that Dick robbed my house, and when they left, they went on the run.

Here is what I have been able to piece together, mostly from news accounts. Sofia and Dick had been in Indiana, at the home of a lawyer named Veronica Fischer, who had represented my ex-wife in our divorce proceedings. I had had no contact with Fischer for quite a long time. She and my ex-wife had claimed that I had failed to pay child support, although I had actually fulfilled my obligations long before that.

I had fired Michael Schmidt, my lawyer at the time, because with all the chaos in my professional career, including moving from the Southwest to Italy and back, I could no longer afford his services. Besides, he had proved incompetent in many areas. As I've been writing this book, I've learned that he never filed modification of child support papers despite the fact that I had not been working. But at the time, I believed the case was open-and-shut enough that I could represent myself in court in the matter.

Much to my surprise, Schmidt screwed me royally. He told me that he *had* filed papers to correct child support issues, although he actually had not. Obviously he was being influenced by Veronica Fischer and the whole conspiracy. In fact, they had probably paid him off, as I learned after being released from the hospital just before he died.

Tragically, nobody was notified about my accident, and in my absence, they fabricated all kinds of stories, trying to point fingers and slander me. The case actually went to court while I was still in a coma. Michael Schmidt was supposed to provide the court with evidence that I had paid child support for my daughter as required, but he never did so. Apparently the court case went on without my presence or knowledge, and then I had to appeal because of their fraudulent actions and lack of notifying me.

Before I dismissed him, Schmidt told me that he had delivered all the evidence to the court. However, I recently found out that he lied to me, abandoning me in my time of crisis and letting these criminals get away with extortion. This leads me to believe that he was part of the extortion scheme.

I only recently acquired transcripts of the court proceedings, whereupon I learned that Fischer and my ex-wife fraudulently stated to the court that I had failed to pay child support. Furthermore, they attempted to exclude $66,000 that I had paid directly to them, arguing that that money had been a gift rather than a child support payment. Why would I have given my ex-wife a gift? I wanted to pay my child support in full, resolving my obligations, and that's what I did. I recently learned that Michael passed away in October 2017, which I guess just proves that karma has no deadline.

While writing this chapter, I was again served with papers by child support services threatening to revoke my passport and medical license, along with other nonsense issues, all of which were fraudulent and have now been resolved. Chelsea's mantra was to destroy me at all costs. She is relentless!

When Sofia was arrested in 2015 while I was in my coma, they found a syringe on her. After she was released, it was tested and found to contain succinylcholine, a drug used by anesthesiologists during surgery. The sheriff's office then issued an arrest warrant for Sofia and Dick, and prosecutors charged them with conspiracy to commit murder.

So many issues surrounding this incident confuse me. Perhaps the most puzzling—to me, anyhow—is the syringe of succinylcholine. I don't know how in God's name she ever got hold of that, and I'm almost willing to believe that Fischer and her co-conspirators planted it. After all, Fischer's husband was a police officer based at the same jail where Sofia was held when she was arrested. Did he plant the syringe?

Succinylcholine is a highly restricted drug. I can't write a prescription for it or even order it for my office. It can be ordered only under the auspices of a hospital by an anesthesiologist, for use in an operating room setting where it's used to paralyze a patient before intubation. There was no way that Sofia or I had access to something so dangerous, but someone else might have. A friend of Dr. Morelli's was the chief of anesthesia at the hospital in Arizona. I can't prove any connection, but it seems much more likely to me that someone connected with Dr. Morelli or Veronica Fischer would have been able to plant drugs on Sofia than that she would have been able to obtain them herself.

Her arrest, as described in court records, on the internet, and in news stories, just didn't sound like the Sofia I knew. Years earlier, I had experienced a falling-out with my father, and then we didn't speak for five or six years—until Sofia made peace between us. In 2012, while I was in Tucson taking a course in integrative medicine, Sofia had contacted my father and convinced him that he and I should reunite. I got a phone call from him, after six years of separation, which she had apparently orchestrated, and that phone call led us to make peace and start communicating with each other again. Whenever we had a disagreement after that, Sofia would call my father and help settle it. That was just the kind of person she was, in my experience.

While writing this book, I received a letter from Helen, Sofia's mother. When she learned that I was writing this book, which would include issues related to her daughter, she became deathly afraid that the lawyers involved with Sofia's case—in particular, Veronica Fischer and Matthew Wiley—would attempt to have her incarcerated daughter assassinated. It's easy to have someone murdered in prison when you have the ability to pay another inmate, either in a barter or with a deal for a reduced sentence. This happens almost monthly in most federal penitentiaries, and it illustrates just how corrupt and dangerous the people who I'm describing in this book are!

The network of organized criminal activity and the collective guilt of the people involved is quite extensive, which is why I'm using the fictitious names *Sofia* Lombardi and *Dick* to refer to this woman and her son. I also want to be clear that the statements I am making are not just speculative; they're based on reading official statements from the people involved in this story.

After reading an appeal Sofia filed in May 2018, there is no question in my mind that she was set up and entrapped by Fischer and Wiley, working with the FBI. Everything that was posted on the internet is garbage. The real story goes like this: When Sofia was in Fort Alexander County Jail, in Indiana, she was seen by a mental health counselor named Rollins.

Mental health counselors are not allowed to prescribe medications; psychiatrists are medical doctors, but a mental health counselor is not. According to her mother, Sofia saw Rollins, a mental health counselor, without the supervision of a medical doctor, and Rollins supplied her with drugs. So you must be wondering, How was that possible? That action alone is illegal, which exemplifies the corruption at hand.

Rollins, apparently for reasons to be made clear later, put her on a medication called Zyprexa (Olanzapine), which belongs to a class of drugs called atypical antipsychotics. These drugs work by helping to restore the balance of certain natural substances in the brain. Zyprexa is a strong medication normally used in treating schizophrenia, and its side effects include impairment of thinking and behavior, restlessness, memory loss, drowsiness, lightheadedness, seizures, and lethargy. And that's exactly what happened to Sofia when she was given Zyprexa.

Sofia began to hallucinate while she was incarcerated with a cellmate named Ana Lopez. Apparently Lopez was working with Fischer and the FBI to entrap me by creating a fictitious scenario, but they couldn't implicate me because I was in a coma, so they had to rethink their strategy. They opted to put Sofia in a pharmacologically induced gullible condition with Zyprexa, causing her to hallucinate and willingly accept any suggestion. Ana Lopez was placed in Sofia's cell for that purpose.

I remember Helen contacting me to tell me that Sofia was hallucinating and falling out of bed after being placed on this medication. Apparently Sofia was not her normal self, talking incoherently, trying to put her hands through walls, and things like that. Rollins was working in conjunction with Fischer, the FBI, and her lawyer Matthew Wiley.

Although he was married, Wiley had a girlfriend named Jennifer Fields. Guess who worked in Jennifer Fields's office?

Yes, Veronica Fischer, my ex-wife's corrupt attorney who has been trying to destroy me for the past decade. Obviously, this was a conflict of interest, so Matthew Wiley should have recused himself from the case.

Both Chelsea and Fischer were relentless in their attacks. Unfortunately, Sofia was collateral damage after their plan to implicate me in the attempted murder of my ex-wife and her attorney fell apart. They realized too late that I was in a coma throughout the time of the alleged incident. So they got Rollins to illegally prescribe Zyprexa to make Sofia hallucinate and leave her open to the power of suggestion. You must understand at this point that mental health counselors that work in prison are not under the auspices of the medical board of Indiana. They are under the guidance of the jail. This was told to the mother as a point of fact. The fact that Wiley never relinquished Rollins's name, severely implicates him in this conspiracy. I guess they never thought that somebody would ever read the FBI transcripts even if I didn't have anything to do with this case. Guess what? You got caught with your hand in the cookie jar.

Sofia's mother repeatedly requested the name of the mental health counselor, but Wiley never provided that information, an act that strongly implicates him and Fischer in this conspiracy. He and Fischer are among many US attorneys who use their law licenses for malicious prosecution and abuse of process. One of my ex-wife's other lawyers, Connor Truman, was found guilty of the same offense: malicious prosecution and abuse of process. I sued him for eight million dollars in Arizona's Mojave County Superior Court in 2018 and won!

Wiley and Fischer offered Ana Lopez a deal to help them implicate Sofia and me in a murder for hire by lying. None of the prior charges of alleged attempted murder that Sofia faced would have held up in court because there was no actual attempt to murder. Therefore, they had to fabricate a new scenario that included direct collusion, and bring murder back into their equation. While Sofia was hallucinating and open to the power of suggestion, Ana created a scenario in which somebody on the outside would be able to assassinate Veronica and Chelsea, following the FBI's instructions.

Helen tried to file a report with the Indiana medical licensing board, but it went nowhere. So much for the state overseeing their licensees. They said that the issue would have to be investigated by Fort Alexander County Jail, where Sofia and Ana had shared a cell.

So much for justice in the state of Indiana! They actually have mental health counselors, for personal gain, illegally prescribing dangerous psychotropic medications for patients. Obviously, Fischer must have paid off Rollins, and Wiley never provided Helen with the names of either Rollins or the psychiatrist who were apparently on the case. This was a scam and entrapment instigated by Rollins, using psychotropic medications as a tool of conspiracy with Fischer and the FBI.

Ana was hired and placed in that cell with Sofia to employ the power of suggestion and whisper in Sofia's ear what to say to implicate herself. Without question, Sofia was under the influence of strong medication that impaired her thought process. While Sofia was hallucinating, Lopez told her that she knew somebody who would be able to take care of Veronica and Chelsea, apparently by murdering them.

In her pharmacologically impaired state, unable to think for herself, Sofia went along with this. So when she received a phone call from this person on the outside, she was told it was a hit man. Ana had suggested that this so-called hit man, whom she called "Dom-Dom," should contact me.

But that makes no sense at all! If this person really was a hit man and Ana was able to orchestrate an assassination attempt, why would I need to be involved unless the intention was to implicate me? That's exactly what their plans were, but they fell apart very quickly.

Of course, I did not want to get involved, and although no words were ever spoken to me about murder, I did not want to have anything to do with the situation. I told Helen at the time that things didn't seem right: "Be careful. This sounds like they're trying to set her up." And that's exactly what they did.

This so-called hit man, who was actually an FBI agent, even contacted me at home and said, "I understand you have some issues with people whom you want to take care of."

"I don't know what you're talking about," I replied, "nor do I want anything to do with this." This was an attempt at entrapment by legal authorities and attorneys, trying to implicate me while giving Ana Lopez a deal, but their plan fell apart.

Sofia was unjustly found guilty of attempted murder for hire. Her appeal was denied, and she's serving a twenty-seven-year sentence. When a person serves time in a federal penitentiary, they must complete at least 80 percent of the sentence before being eligible for parole, so Sofia will have to serve at least twenty-one years.

This shows clearly just how corrupt the legal and medical systems in Indiana are. The lawyers, Rollins, and the FBI entrapped this poor woman by pharmacologically breaking down her mind. They made a case out of lies and deception, and they intentionally and illegally drugged her until she went along with their story. The transcripts show that Sofia and Ana Lopez (a known criminal) were in contact with each other, as well as Matthew Wiley and the FBI, before this event, thus giving clear indications of entrapment.

Rollins, the mental health counselor, should be formally investigated, and the phone records of his conversations with Veronica Fischer should be subpoenaed. These steps would enlighten the world about these corrupt actions and allow justice to be served.

I believe that after our breakup, Sofia wanted to get back into my good graces. She had come to visit me in Italy, where I had performed pelvic reconstructive surgery on her. She also had helped with some transportation issues when I was returning to the United States to work for Dr. Nassif. So it's easy for me to think that she was trying to help me out by attempting to get Fischer off my back. Sofia knew that the people allied against me could and would destroy my career, and perhaps she believed she was in a position to save me from that fate. Deep down she's a kind, thoughtful person, and it's genuinely sad that she became a victim of the conspiracy against me.

It says a great deal about Sofia as a friend and a person of integrity that she never allowed me to be implicated in anything she and Dick did. Many people would have loved to find a way to tie me to anything nefarious, but Sofia never brought my name into it. For that and her friendship, I will always be grateful.

CHAPTER SEVEN

The Cover-Up

While I was hospitalized, a stream of doctors were in and out of my room. Even when I was conscious, I really didn't make an effort to remember them. But I do recall telling the nurses that under no circumstances was Dr. Nassif to be allowed into my room or given any information about my condition or treatment.

It should be obvious why I gave this order. The man had left me to die! And while he never did come into my room or attempt to speak with me during my recovery, he nevertheless was given information about my treatment and prognosis. One day, I saw him in the hallway talking with Dr. Methani, my primary care physician. Methani was talking to Nassif about me, and breaking HIPAA confidentiality rules in the process. I overheard Nassif ask, "So do you really think that he's going to make it through this process without any residual sequela?" I think Nassif was terrified that I would survive. Guess what, I did! And I still have not forgotten your criminal behavior that amounted to attempted murder.

It's illegal for a physician to breach a patient's right to confidentiality with any other nontreating physician, but Methani and Nassif were close friends. So Methani shared my information with Nassif, showing no regard for his own legal responsibilities or my safety. At that stage of my recovery, I didn't want to bring it up with my doctor, for fear that he might have chosen to allow the situation to have negative repercussions on my care and treatment.

That was not the end of Dr. Methani's treachery. When I was coming out of my coma and still highly disoriented, I asked him to write a letter to my attorney informing him that I was hospitalized in critical condition. Without explanation, Methani refused to do so. My attorney in Indiana, where I was still fighting my divorce case, had told me that he needed that letter to put to rest Veronica Fischer's false claim that I had not paid child support. It was as if Methani was conspiring with Fischer.

Fortunately, there was no evidence to support Fischer's claim and plenty of evidence that I had in fact fulfilled my financial obligations to my ex-wife and children. But that evidence was fraudulently tampered with and tainted by Veronica Fischer in a trial that I was not notified about and did not attend.

In May 2015, while I was still in intensive care, I received a phone call from my oldest child and only son, Vincenzo. A handsome man in his thirties, Vincenzo has my physical characteristics—a beautiful face and brown eyes, good physical shape, brown hair, five foot eleven, and a beard like mine. He lived in Miami and was traveling to New York at the time, but his trip was barely underway. He wasn't even in Jacksonville yet when I received his call.

"Hey, Dad, how are you doing?" he asked.

I said, "Vincenzo, I've been in a coma. I'm still critically ill and don't know if I'll survive this hospitalization. Are you coming to see me?"

"We've been driving all day, Dad, and we're headed for New York. I have friends in the car with me, and we really have to be in New York within a day."

"This is disappointing, Vincenzo," I replied. "You do realize that you may never again see your father alive, don't you?"

Vincenzo did not even have the decency to travel three hours out of his way to visit his father, who was in a state of near death. To this day, I haven't forgiven him. Regardless of the sacrifices you make for your children, when push comes to shove, they'll put their friends ahead of their own parents.

Meanwhile my daughter, who lives in Nebraska, had been emancipated in June 2015 at nineteen years of age and was making fraudulent statements to my own mother that I was somehow involved in Sofia's arrest in Indiana. She also did not know that I was in the ICU on my deathbed. I knew nothing about what was going on with her. How could I have known, trapped in my own house and later in a hospital?

I never treated my own father so disrespectfully. As I mentioned earlier, we had been estranged for many years, before Sofia interceded and helped us make peace. Even when we were apart, though, I had respect for my father. When he was in critical condition in 2005, I flew from the Midwest to be at his bedside. I helped make life decisions for him, which ultimately brought him an extra thirteen years of life. I always had respect for my father!

I will say this: about a year and a half ago June 2016, my daughter called me, after not speaking to me for more than a decade. She wanted to apologize for all the lies she had fabricated with my ex-wife during the divorce testimony. She had become a born-again Christian and was about to be baptized into her new faith, which required her to gain forgiveness from people she had sinned against.

When she called me, I said, "Natasha, I could and will forgive you, because you are my daughter. But you need to look at this with God and ask yourself why you did such a horrible thing." We've been in communication since that time, rebuilding our relationship.

As if Nassif's attempt to kill me in June 2015 wasn't enough, he betrayed me again after speaking to Methani about my condition. He must have been worried that I would recover, though not because I would press attempted murder charges against him, since the authorities were on his side, as I would find out later. His problem was that if I lived, he would have to honor our employment contract. With his business in shambles from his incompetence and misunderstanding of the market, that was something he couldn't accept. No sooner had I told the nursing staff and security that Dr. Nassif was not allowed to have contact with me than the following happened.

He sent a certified letter to my home, knowing full well that I was still in the intensive care unit. The letter stated that he was firing me, effective immediately, because of my lack of hospital privileges. I had forty-eight hours to remove all my medical equipment from his office, or he would charge me a daily rate of five hundred dollars for rental of office space! Can you believe the audacity of the man? Naturally, he got no response, as my friend Helen had not yet arrived, and the letter was eventually returned to him. We had no way of knowing what was going on.

Helen was in her mid-seventies, rather thin with brown hair and eyes. She had a visual deficiency from a corneal Lasix surgery that had gone badly and damaged the retina in her left eye, but she was smart as a whip and a kind, warmhearted person.

Helen arrived on a Tuesday. Maria, my office manager, had told her that I was going to have open-heart surgery in the afternoon, but she didn't know the exact time. Helen drove straight through from her home, in Arizona, not even bothering to stop at night or rest. She knew that if she didn't get to see me before the surgery, she might not have a chance to talk to me at all, ever again. The odds of making it through the operation in my condition were dismal.

Upon her arrival, she rushed up to my room. Shortly afterward, when one of my doctors came into my room, Helen asked about the surgery.

"He won't be having any surgery today," said the physician.

The next day, I was literally being wheeled to the operating room for open-heart valve replacement when the internal medicine/cardiologist/infectious disease specialist decided to run one more test. It was something he had checked just a week before, but he wanted it done again, just to be sure. The test revealed that the damage to my heart valve had repaired itself, so surgery was unnecessary. It was a miracle!

Helen not only cared for me in the hospital, but also retrieved my mail and paid bills that otherwise would have been overdue. She stayed at my house, and I could count on her to visit me every day. She would read my mail to me at my bedside, and we would make decisions about things that required attention.

When the certified letter didn't have the desired effect, Nassif had his attorney send me an email. What kind of maniac would expect a man in ICU to be reading email? Fortunately Helen read the email to me, though I was still in a confused state in the intensive care unit. I remember her growing more livid with every word she read. She called Nassif a son of a bitch and God knows what else.

> Please accept this letter as formal notice of termination of the agreement, for cause, effective June 9, 2015.
>
> Pursuant to section 10.8 of the agreement, the agreement may be terminated for cause without prior notice for numerous reasons including if you involuntarily lose or have restrictions placed upon the privilege of performing medical services in any hospital … Due to your inability to obtain privileges at the hospital we are terminating the agreement, for cause, pursuant to section 10.8 of the agreement, etc.

To make a long story short, not only was my employment terminated, but I was to remove my belongings—urological equipment, medical books, and everything else from my office—immediately, or he would begin charging me five hundred dollars a day for storage. In addition, he would bill me for the cost of having my things moved to storage. It was insane! He knew I was in the hospital and incapacitated, but he fired me and then demanded that I pay him five hundred dollars a day to store medical instruments I had brought from Italy for use in his facility. It was one of the most pathetic, dishonest things I had ever seen.

There was obviously no way anyone could make arrangements to have all that stuff moved within the period stipulated by Nassif and his crooked lawyer. From my hospital bed, I dictated an email that Helen typed for me, stating that if I was not given a reasonable period of time to have my belongings moved, I would report Nassif and his attorney to the Medical Board in a "Standard of Care" report.

CHAPTER EIGHT

The Criminal

Helen had been in Florida for about a week. She was living in my house and driving my car.

After Helen and I responded to Dr. Nassif's email, she was told by Nassif that she could go to the office the following Monday at ten o'clock to claim my personal paperwork, medical books, framed educational documents, and other items. She arrived at the agreed-upon time, only to be told that no one was there to unlock the office for her. So Helen returned home, but then Nassif's staff called and asked her to return at one o'clock. They did not care that it was a fifteen-mile trip to the office and back; in fact, they obviously wanted everything to be as irritating and inconvenient for her as possible.

Helen returned at one o'clock and was kept waiting again. Finally she was escorted into my private office, where someone had thrown my framed diplomas, paperwork, and various other items into garbage cans. Maria and Courtney, my office manager and nurse, had been told that they would be fired if they set foot in my office again.

Helen had just managed to get everything loaded into the car when one of Dr. Nassif's employees, who was overseeing her without helping in any way, told her that all the medical books in the cabinet behind the desk belonged to me as well. So she carried every single book out to the car, until every inch of space was filled.

She then asked when it would be possible to return and start packing up the smaller items for the moving company. She was told to return at one o'clock the next day, and that again someone would be with her at all times as she was packing.

That night Helen unpacked the car, carrying the medical books, framed diplomas and certifications, and various folders from my desk into the house. In a folder labeled "Contracts," which I had put in my desk before leaving for New Orleans, there should have been three separate contracts: one pertaining to the setup of the corporation, one pertaining to the salary Nassif was to pay me, and the last and most recent pertaining to the rental agreement for the medical equipment. That third contract was missing, even though Nassif's office manager had told Helen that it had been there just a day or two before she packed everything up.

When Helen returned the next day, there was no one to let her in. She was told by the receptionist that Dr. Nassif would arrive shortly and that he would go through the exam rooms with her to discuss what was to be taken and what belonged to him.

When Dr. Nassif arrived, he greeted Helen cordially. Before he could begin shepherding her through the office, however, she immediately brought up the missing contract. He was standing with one of his technicians, Erica, and Helen addressed them both.

"I unpacked the supplies I picked up yesterday," she said, "and I found that one of the contracts is missing. It's the one that has to do with the rental of the medical equipment and disposables, and it should have been in the same folder as the other two parts of the contract. I was told that Erica did the packing, so I assume that she took it."

Nassif stared at Helen. The audacity of this woman, coming into his office and accusing one of his employees of stealing! He turned to Erica and asked, "Did you take the contract that Helen is talking about?"

"No, I didn't see it," Erica replied. "Perhaps Maria or Courtney took it, since they did most of the packing."

This was a lie, of course, since Maria and Courtney had been ordered not to set foot in my office. It was obvious that

Dr. Nassif had stolen my copy of the contract to cover up his activities.

"That's quite a serious charge," Nassif said to Helen. "Why would you say such a thing?"

"One of the women here told me that Erica took it," Helen replied calmly.

"Who was it?" demanded Nassif.

"Oh, I'm sorry, I have no idea. You know, I just arrived from Arizona, and I'm quite turned around when it comes to names or even where everything is," Helen told him innocently. "Well, shall we get this tour done so I can get my work done?"

Nassif could easily have offered to make a copy of the contract from his own files, but he didn't. It was obvious that he intended to avoid paying the $6,000 monthly fee for the equipment. He was five months late on those payments. This was blatantly criminal behavior.

As they entered each exam room, Nassif agreed that the contents of the cabinets belonged to me. Helen said she'd been told that the disposables, which were mostly stored in cabinets outside the laboratory, had all been brought from Italy. Nassif disagreed, though, saying, "No, all the supplies in the storage area outside the laboratory are mine." That was a lie.

Helen decided to just let it go, since she had no way of proving anything and nobody to back her up. It would have to be dealt with in court after I had recovered.

By then it was nearly three in the afternoon and Helen had only two hours left to pack boxes. She spent that time marking, counting, and categorizing the catheters. There were literally hundreds of them, enough to fill a huge packing box, and Nassif had instructed his employee to mark and photograph each item, making it all very time consuming.

Helen was told that she could come back the next morning at eight and stay until noon. It was already Tuesday, and she had contracted professional movers to move the equipment between one and five on Friday afternoon.

On Wednesday morning, Helen showed up at eight, and again Nassif had assigned two girls to stay with her the entire time. It seemed like a ridiculous level of security for equipment that belonged to me anyway. What did they think she would steal? The exam tables were mine, but how would she lift one, get it out of the building, and fit it into her car? It was an absurd attempt at intimidation by Nassif, but it didn't work.

Nassif continued working against Helen in other ways. Every day, if Helen had been told to be there at eight, she would arrive only to be told they had changed it to one o'clock, although they never bothered to phone and let her know. But Thursday was the final day and there was little left to pack, even as they changed their minds over and over about what was mine and what was his.

Helen finished packing the last few boxes and told the two employees supervising her that she would see them the next afternoon as agreed. Friday was to be moving day, and the movers would arrive around one thirty.

One of the girls said, "Oh, I'm sorry, but we've changed the time to eight o'clock until noon. We have patients coming in during the afternoon."

"Well, with such short notice, I don't know if the moving company will be able to accommodate the time change," Helen responded. "But I'll see you at eight o'clock tomorrow morning and see what can be done."

Helen called the moving company immediately. They said they would do what they could, but schedules were already in place and they could not promise that they could find the manpower to suddenly switch from afternoon to morning.

Helen came to the hospital each day after the packing portion was finished, and it was disappointing to hear how difficult they were making things for her. Unfortunately, there was nothing I could do. Each day was a battle just to stay alive, and it took all my energy to focus on staying positive and try to get through the day. I was going through dialysis, and the neuropathy was causing severe pain in my legs. There were times when I just wished it would all end, and I still question why God did not take me the day I died. Obviously he has other plans for me.

Helen said to me, "Dr. Panvini, I don't know how you could've survived this horrendous ordeal if I had not driven to Florida from Arizona for you. This man Dr. Nassif is a horrible human being, and I hope you don't let him get away with attempted murder."

"If not for you, Helen, I don't know what I would've done," I told her. "You see me here in this intensive care unit bed, unable to walk or concentrate on a task because of my recent coma. I want to thank you from the bottom of my heart for everything that you are doing for me. God bless you."

Finally, thanks to Helen, I was able to get my equipment out of Dr. Nassif's office and wash my hands of that horrible criminal once and for all.

CHAPTER NINE

The Move from Italy

You might be wondering why I did not file legal charges against Dr. Nassif. After all, he had fired me without cause, broken my employment contract, acted in a thoroughly unprofessional manner, and even tried to murder me! And believe me, if I'd had the money to spare, I would definitely have sued him. The problem was that I was broke. After signing a good contract with Nassif, I had been starting to make serious money as my local reputation grew, but I also had a lot of legal bills. Money was going right back out as fast as it arrived.

My problems also extended beyond the professional arena. Emotionally distraught, I was at the lowest point of my life. I thought I'd never walk again, my career was in ruins, and when I started to look on the internet and see all the garbage that was out there, I sank even deeper into despair.

With Helen at my bedside, helping me search for my name on the internet, our conversation would go like this: "Helen, I can't believe all this crap that's on the internet about me. How can they make these types of allegations when I was in the hospital in a coma?" There were allegations about me conspiring to murder my ex-wife, her attorney, and my daughter. Why would I ever contemplate murdering my daughter, ex-wife, *anybody*?

Helen would respond, "You're not dealing with normal people. These are vicious people who have no morals or conscience. They will do anything to destroy you and your professional career, and it appears that they're succeeding. They are also ostracizing you from all your friends and family deliberately. It's a shame to see you emotionally distraught from this trauma and the stuff on the internet while you're still trying to get better."

"Helen," I said, "you know that I'm a fighter. I never give up!"

Searching for my name in Google brought up page after page of unbelievable garbage, and I had to address each person posting these false allegations and threaten them with a lawsuit. I did that to clean up the nonsense that was being falsely alleged on the internet, such as this:

> Suburban Indianapolis authorities say a Florida woman and her son are believed to be on the lam after they failed to appear in court to face

charges alleging they plotted to kill a divorce attorney seeking money from the woman's boyfriend.

Arrest warrants issued Friday in Hamilton Superior Court charge 51-year-old Sofia Lombardi, of Florida, and 21-year-old Dick Lombardi, of Laughlin, Nevada, with conspiracy to commit murder and other counts.

The *Indianapolis Star* reports they were released on $20,000 bonds paid by Dr. Panvini, May 23 after being arrested on lesser charges outside the Noblesville home of attorney Veronica Fischer. Fischer was pursuing unpaid settlement money from Dr. Dino Panvini of Arizona, on behalf of his ex-wife.

Interestingly, these postings all originated from Indianapolis, where Veronica Fischer practiced. Fortunately, the people posting this garbage didn't know that I had few resources to devote to the struggle to save my reputation. I was lucky that almost everyone took down their fraudulent posts about me, realizing they had placed themselves in a legally vulnerable position.

I wrote numerous emails to these news agencies:

Your news article on the internet is factually incorrect and is defamatory, as it is interfering with my ability to practice medicine and obstructing my trade. I had nothing to do with these actions. Your article is fake news that has been propagated through a conspiracy action and is responsible for propagating the initial news source to other sites.

I urge you to remove my name from your internet posting as soon as possible, as it has interfered with my ability to practice medicine and it has damaged my reputation under false pretense. Please remove my name from your above article as soon as possible before legal action is taken. If you wish for me to elaborate on the entire case, I would be most happy to do so. Please email me if you are interested in an interview.

The news article to which I am referring is as follows: "Dr. Panvini alleged implication in attempted murder plot of ex-wife's attorney with Miss. Lombardi and son"

I even hired an internet company to try to bury some of the fraudulent postings against me by putting them farther down on the search results. Either way, I had to consult an attorney in Indiana and retain him for his services, though he was paid handsomely for doing nothing. What a waste of money!

Only a few of these false stories remain online, mostly from small Indiana newspapers that obviously have alliances with Veronica Fischer to propagate fraud. However, some information had even circulated internationally. For example, one story came from a UK-based site, because people knew I had lived in Europe for several years. They were trying to poison my reputation internationally to keep me from returning. I believe these stories originated with Veronica Fischer, who fed them to the local Indiana papers and then to other people and news outlets through an approach similar to the AP newswire, a service for which she paid. Fischer, my ex-wife's attorney, was fulfilling my ex-wife's prophecy by damaging my reputation in any way, shape, or form. Fortunately I've been able to salvage my reputation, rebuilding it just as I am rebuilding my life.

At this point, I will explain the full story of my time in Italy, and how I came to be involved with Nassif and his cronies. I had moved to Italy from Fort Mojave, Arizona, where I had been threatened out of practicing medicine, as I described earlier. I reached out to my father and some other relatives to help me decide what to do.

Before speaking to them, I had taken my grievances to the Arizona hospital authorities in February 2013, expecting them to intervene since I was the chairman of surgery at the time. Dr. Morelli had been kicked out of the hospital in 2012, literally escorted off the grounds by the police, because he was a crazy son of a bitch and everyone in town knew it. He was prohibited from ever again setting foot on any property owned by the parent company, Careline Health. I had struck a major blow against Morelli and his corrupt operation, reporting him to the federal government under a "qui tam" whistleblower action, and thus I was afraid for my life.

I asked the hospital administration to help me out, because they knew exactly what was going on with Morelli and his conspiracy against my professional career and office personnel. To say they were unhelpful would be a major understatement. After what I considered an unreasonably protracted discussion, they finally made an offer to buy all of my instruments, as well as those leased to me by Sofia. This was an attempt to have Sofia reimbursed for her losses. As you will recall, she had become a silent investor in my practice to help keep me afloat in the wake of attempts by Dr. Morelli and his thugs to drive me under.

The hospital's offer was an insult; they wanted to pay pennies on the dollar for the instruments. I had bigger problems, though. I asked again, "How are you going to protect me?" When I didn't get a satisfactory answer, I told them, "You've got a month to think about it and give me an answer."

During that month I was paranoid and fearful, living like a hunted man. I lived in a house in Laughlin whose owner agreed to put all the utilities, cable, electricity, and so on in his name so that I couldn't be tracked down by my enemy. I hired a bodyguard (ex–Navy Seal) to follow me to and from work and an armed ex–police officer to file paperwork in my office.

One month later, I went back to the hospital administration and told them, "I'm in private practice. I can leave any time I want, and I'm not going to put up with life-threatening situations if you're not going to protect me. Find yourself another chief of surgery and urologist. Goodbye." Then I resigned and left. Packing up my life to move to Italy took some time, but by September 2013 I was ready to move to the country of my ancestors, where I had lots of relatives and friends.

While waiting for the administration to get back to me, I had asked my father what he would do in my shoes. He had said, "You have angered a wasps' nest and pissed off a lot of dangerous people, so you need to go to a safe place. I know a lot of people in Italy, where you have many relatives. You can trust those people wholeheartedly, and some of them are in high positions of authority in the Italian government." He had proposed the idea of moving to Italy, where I had studied medicine for many years. Also he had a lot of friends in Italy with whom he could set me up, so ultimately it was an easy decision.

When I got to Italy, I again went off the map, as they say, by renting an apartment from one of my relatives in Italy, where everything was paid for under their name and I could reimburse them. I was in Torino, Italy's fourth-largest city, an ancient metropolis on the banks of the Po River that's flanked by the Alps. Civilization in the region dates back to before the year 200 BC, and Torino (also known as Turin) was the first capital city of the unified Kingdom of Italy in 1861.

My uncle was a high-ranking official in the Italian police department, so he made sure I was secure. I began laying the foundation for what could have been a good life there in February 2014. I was still licensed to practice medicine in Italy, from when I had studied there years earlier, although toward the end of my stay, they changed the laws and I had to go through the application process all over again. Still, I was getting ready to practice medicine under the auspices of the University of Rome, lecturing there and setting up a private office, when once again it seemed like fate was determined to strike me down.

One day in May, I slipped on a wet cobblestone street and fell. At the local hospital, I learned that I had a herniated cervical disc in my neck. I was in excruciating pain, and my right arm was basically rendered useless. I was forced to wear a neck brace and keep my arm elevated.

The workup consisted of MRIs and other testing, as well as a regimen of physical therapy before I could have the necessary surgery. The physical therapy was nonsense and did nothing to alleviate my chronic pain or restore mobility or utility to my neck or arm. The pain in my right arm was unrelenting despite the medications that I was given, which I did not tolerate well, especially the narcotics.

As summer dragged on, I was on a waiting list for surgery, and then August came around and everyone disappeared. People joke about how Europe empties out in August, and it's true. But when you're waiting to have a medical procedure that will enable you to resume your professional life, after having literally been chased out of your home country, celebrating Ferragosto isn't fun.

It wasn't until October that I finally had my operation. After I had recovered, I decided to move from Torino to Rome, where I set up a clinic and lectured at the University of Rome. I started working on a new department that would focus on female urogynecology, laser surgery, and integrative medicine, a subject on which I had done my fellowship.

Integrative medicine takes into account the full range of influences on a person's health; physical, emotional, mental, social, spiritual, and environmental factors are all considered. The doctor and patient develop a personalized strategy that considers the patient's unique needs, as well as the circumstances surrounding their illness and—just as importantly—the rest of their life. Both alternative methods and conventional medicine are used not only to heal the immediate illness, but also to help people regain and maintain their best possible health. Health is much more than simply not being sick; it involves every aspect of a person's life. Integrative medicine takes as many factors as possible into account to make patients truly healthy, rather than just telling them, "You're not sick anymore, so here's my bill."

I was also pioneering urological surgical techniques, showing my fellow physicians practices that had been done in the United States but were not yet common in Italy. Sofia came to see me so that I could perform on her an outpatient surgical procedure that was still unheard of over there. I had an audience in the operating theater just to see how I did things.

Had I stayed in Rome, I would've helped build a new division of urology at the University of Rome that would have included urogynecology as well as surgical procedures that help put people back together. Urologists in Italy were not doing that like they were in the United States, and some Italian gynecologists were doing real damage to their patients. Everything was looking up for me. I was also trained in urogynecology, unlike Italian urologists. Female reconstructive work was done only by gynecologists, who didn't help their patients the right way, resulting in a lot of recurrences. So I was doing pelvic organ prolapse surgery on women who had been operated on previously, with fabulous results and satisfied patients.

In November 2014, when I was on the brink of signing a contract with the University of Rome, I received an invitation from Nassif in Florida. Needing a competent urologist to augment his practice, he had looked through my background and thought I could be just the guy for the job. I flew to

Resort City Beach, liked the area, and instead of taking a professorship at the University of Rome School of Medicine and Surgery and setting up a new program there, I took the job with Nassif.

My decision to return to the United States might seem like a huge mistake, even bizarre. Looking back now, I believe that Nassif might have working with Connor Truman and Veronica Fischer to get me back to the United States.

Ultimately, it was the financial enticements that led me back. In Italy, medicine is divided into the private sector and the socialized sector. The universities are part of the socialized medicine program, which is extremely widespread. I had to deal with it personally when I was waiting months for my neck operation. And working for the university in Rome, I wouldn't have been paid for procedures the way I would be in the United States. It was only through private practice that I would have been able to make any real money, but I never had the chance to get a private practice off the ground, so I was still struggling financially under the weight of legal bills and other expenses. I had legal expenses from Connor Truman's false malpractice allegations, attorneys that I had to pay for bankruptcy issues, attorneys that I had to pay for managing fraudulent statements to Arizona's medical licensing board and the Department of Health and Human Resources, divorce lawyers, and so on.

Nassif's offer was generous—a base annual salary of $600,000, plus an incentive program through which I would receive 60 percent of whatever else I brought in. There would also be the income from the medical supplies I would provide to the practice. It was a lot of money, and would have allowed me to live a comfortable life.

If only he hadn't been a criminal.

CHAPTER TEN

Mycell

I was a twenty-three-year-old American student in Italy in June 1973. It was a warm summer and I had just arrived in Naples to attend medical school. We have been doctors in our family since the 1500s, all graduating from Italian medical schools. My father graduated from the University of Naples, and I wanted to carry on the family tradition of attending medical school. I was totally confused, however, and my first day of classes was complete chaos. I didn't know any Italian, so I was at a loss as to how to learn anything. Not only were the tests in Italian, but I would have to sit before a panel of professors and take oral exams in Italian. I had a lot of work ahead of me!

I thought that the best strategy would be to live with someone local, and I was lucky enough to find a family with a room to rent just down the street from the medical school. They had a good-looking daughter, which made my decision much easier! She needed to learn English, and I needed to learn Italian. She knew nothing about medicine, but I decided to get a tape recorder and learn through conversation.

I was on a tight budget; with an annual five-thousand-dollar student loan, I had to pay for medical books, rent, and food. Electronic equipment was expensive, and tape recorders cost more than two hundred dollars! But I finally found one at a street stand in a neighborhood called Forcella, which I didn't know was much like New York's Harlem. I bargained with the gentleman, finally striking a deal for fifty dollars. He put the tape recorder in a box, wrapped it up in paper, and we made the exchange. I took several buses back to my apartment, thinking I had just saved a hundred and fifty dollars.

The signora of the house and her daughter followed me into my room, where I placed the box on my desk and opened it. To my amazement, it was full of rocks and paper! What had happened? The mother and daughter were laughing hysterically, and I began to laugh too. I'd been ripped off! The guy was a master, to have pulled such a trick right before my eyes, but he was in trouble now!

I couldn't persuade anyone to return to that bad neighborhood with me until I phoned a fellow American named Scott. We were both first-year medical students and New Yorkers. We took the bus to the center of Naples and proceeded to walk endless miles, searching each and every piazza including the spot where I had first met the thief, but he was nowhere to be found. By five o'clock we were totally exhausted, with blisters on our feet from walking God knows how many miles. We were just about to give up and try to find a bus. Then I looked across the piazza and there he was—the man who had ripped me off, talking with several of his friends, probably telling them how he had robbed me.

Filled with adrenaline and rage, I rushed toward him with nothing but a short black tote umbrella in my right hand—but he knew I meant business. Before I got my hands on him, he quickly said in Italian, "I don't have your money," and pulled out his pants pockets.

I grabbed him by his shirt and pinned him up against the wall, waving my umbrella under his nose like a baton. I could see the fright in his eyes as I started yelling, "Give me back my money now!"

Then about thirty of his friends, who were obviously in the same type of business, began to circle around us. My friend Scott was behind me, and he said in English, "Dino, we are going to die. Let's get out of here!"

We were definitely outnumbered, but I decided the best defense was a good offense. I continued yelling and threatening him, shoving the umbrella under his nose and threatening to beat the living daylights out of him. I was terrified, but adrenaline had my heart pumping about a thousand beats per minute.

Scott continued to yell, "Let's get out of here!" as more locals circled us. But suddenly, several of them approached and placed 500- and 1,000-lira bills on the ground by the man's feet. To my amazement, more and more money hit the ground until there was a pile of bills at our feet. I let the man down off the wall, and slowly and carefully he picked up the money and counted it. He placed 50,000 lira in my left hand while I kept the umbrella in my right. I tucked the money into my shirt pocket, and then Scott and I ran for our lives, out of the piazza and down a string of side streets, trying to lose the crowd of people who were chasing us. This was after the man whom I had threatened with an umbrella touched it, realized that it was an umbrella and not a police baton, and said, "Son of a bitch. Get them!"

After running what felt like about five miles in less than a minute, Scott and I ended up in a neighborhood that neither of us recognized. We bent over, hands on our knees, trying to catch our breath and looking around to make sure that we hadn't been followed.

Exhausted and hyperventilating, we approached a newsstand to ask for directions home. The young man who ran the stand came out of his booth and approached me while giving us directions. He pointed with his left hand, explaining that we were to take this bus to such-and-such location and then change to another bus. As he was pointing with his left hand, his right hand was slowly trying to get into my shirt pocket where I had put the money for which I had just risked my life! That son of a bitch was trying to pick my pocket!

When I realized what he was doing, I looked him straight in the eyes and then jumped on top of him. With my knee to his chest and my hands around his throat, I had so much rage in me that I might have killed the man. Scott pulled me away, and the guy got up rubbing his neck, yelling obscenities at me, and telling me I was crazy. When I approached him with the umbrella, getting ready to hit him, he ran back into his booth and pleaded with us to leave him alone.

Scott and I looked at each other and then walked slowly toward the bus stop. Amazed that we were still alive, we shook our heads and laughed hysterically.

I remember thinking that if this was just the first week of medical school, I didn't know how I would survive the next six years. But then I told myself, *I'm tough, and I can handle this and anything else life has to throw at me.*

This is just one of the memories I have of my time studying in Italy. I remember it clearly because of the way my psyche operates, something I recalled while I was in my coma. Life is a composite of what I call *mycells*: tiny translucent clouds filled with enormous amounts of data, faces compiled and saved from various experiences, emotions, and feelings that each of us experiences on our journey through life. These mycells are attracted into our minds for one reason or another, and there they form components of our personality and subconscious.

When we are younger and less experienced, few mycells are present to make up our personality or our emotional road map. We build up more and more mycells as we grow older and cross paths with various people, registering the different aspects of other people's personalities, whether good or bad. These experiences start to accumulate within our minds, as though small bricks compose the walls of a house where all of this information is stored.

As we journey through life, our experiences become more plentiful. Our minds are like sponges, soaking up the information our environment presents to us, as well as our personal experiences with other people. Some of these experiences become treasured memories, or what I would call pearls (a composite of mycells), which accumulate within our minds and become the treasure chest of our true secrets of life.

These pearls linger deep in our subconscious minds and never really surface unless we want them to. At that point, they become part of our conscious mind. Imagine, for example, that you are in a serene, peaceful, and tranquil environment, looking up at the stars on a clear night. Perhaps you start to focus on a particular constellation or even one star. This single star can be thought of as a mycell, and it will trigger your mind if you let it. The constellation of stars is the "pearl."

When we allow them to do so, our minds start to drift, imagining different experiences, people, and encounters that we've had in our lives. Many times, these pearls surface as pleasant memories when we're daydreaming, and they place a smile on our faces.

We meet so many people throughout our lives, never imagining the effect that some encounters may have on our lives as mycells. So we go through our daily routines, day in and day out, accumulating experiences and encounters just as a computer accumulates gigabytes of data. Still, the data accumulated may not be stored in its proper location until the proper environmental structure exists. Think of it like a chemical reaction that creates a molecule out of different atoms.

I imagine this reaction creating a translucent cloud wherein these mycells are stored. Each mycell can contain billions of megabytes of information, stored within a minuscule section of our brain and sometimes coalescing with other mycells to form a compact unit. Then comes the reorganization, when some mycells may be stored within the intellectual portion of our brain, while others may be stored within the emotional or limbic part. Many mycells are the equivalent of random access memory, never tapped into and never resurfacing in our conscious mind.

Now imagine how we live as adults with all these mycells accumulating within our minds. Many are randomly accessed and never stored in a searchable way, though they contain precious information that we can use when we encounter a particular person or when a circumstance stimulates a mystical chemical reaction that forms into a new mycell—or even a pearl! The next time our minds access that information, a pearl presents itself with more dramatic life experiences, and for the first time in our lives, we awaken our conscious minds and experience warm emotional tranquility.

During my near-death experience, in May 2015, I had a vision of these mycells. I felt as though I was floating, and these translucent clouds of mycells were floating past me. I could see into each mycell and reach out to touch them at will. When I inserted my hand into a mycell, the experience that was stored within rushed into my mind and it was as if I was living it all over again, with emotions, smells, sounds, touch, happiness, vision, and so on. People say that when you die, your life passes before your eyes. In some way, having access to so many memories of my life before the accident helped to fortify my belief that I would come out of my coma, recover from the trauma, and get out from under all the attempts my enemies had made to destroy me.

I knew that I would be back.

CHAPTER ELEVEN

Chelsea, the Psychopath

My father was a surgeon, like his father's father before him. Ours has been a family of doctors in Italy since the 1500s. Although I was born and grew up in America, I chose to go to medical school in Italy to keep our family tradition alive. Also, to be honest, it's a lot cheaper to go to medical school in Italy than it is in the United States. Medical school in the United States can cost a quarter of a million dollars, but my tuition in Italy was a tiny fraction of that amount—only a thousand dollars year.

Medical education in Italy is also of much better quality than in the United States. For one thing, strictly in terms of book knowledge, you have to know everything in Italy or you won't pass. The exams are all oral; you stand in front of a panel of about a dozen professors, all staring at you from the other side of a long wooden table, and they go down the line and ask you questions. If you successfully make it to the end of the table, you pass and they give you your score. But if you're not able to answer some questions, you fail and have to come back later and try again. This is different from US medical schools, where you're given written exams with the answers in front of you in a multiple choice format.

I failed none of my classes in Italy and always got high scores. When I finished medical school, I worked at a university medical center, commonly known as a teaching hospital, in Brooklyn. From there I went to Yale, and then I studied urologic surgery at a university in the Midwest.

I met Chelsea, my ex-wife, while I was doing my urological residency at the University of Nebraska Medical Center. I had no idea what I was in for or how she would wreak havoc in my life.

Chelsea was illiterate; she had dyslexia and could barely read or write. When I met her, she was working as a go-go dancer and almost destitute. I felt sorry for her, so I tried to help her learn to read and overcome some of her other issues. We dated for a while during my residency, and then when we moved to New York, I hired the best tutors to teach her how to read and write.

Having finished my surgical residency, I left the state on June 30 and drove straight across the country, intending to go into private practice in New York City, sharing office space with my father. Chelsea came with me as my girlfriend.

I couldn't wait to get out of the Midwest. The winters there were horrendous, sometimes reaching what felt like ninety degrees below zero. It was the kind of cold where you walk outside and it feels like the wind is tearing the skin off your face. At times I would shower and then head for my car before my beard and mustache were fully dry. Just in the short distance between the house and my car, the wind was strong and cold enough to make them freeze. When I touched my beard, pieces of it broke off. I had to keep my car plugged in with a block heater overnight to keep the gas from freezing in the tank. Many times the hospital sent helicopters to pick up residents who were unable to drive to work in their frozen cars.

My relationship with Chelsea wasn't like a boyfriend and girlfriend; it was more like sex with possible future strings. Still, I let her accompany me to New York. Little did I know ...

Chelsea was not a city girl, to put it mildly. She was an uncultured redneck woman with a vulgar mouth, and she had been raised in a house full of guns. She never drove outside her comfort zone, but somehow she acclimated to Long Island. Chelsea dazzled my mother by being at her beck and call, even staying at her house every day while I was at work. My mother was so impressed that she actually persuaded me to marry Chelsea, which I hadn't intended to do. But I was so busy setting up my practice that I agreed without really thinking about it. My mother liked her, and I was a good Italian boy who listened to his mother, so why not?

We married in June 1988, and our son, Vincenzo, was born the following year. Only after he was born did a series of incidents show me who Chelsea really was.

In addition to being functionally illiterate, Chelsea had a temper that would not quit. Whenever someone would use big words around Chelsea, it would frustrate the hell out of her, because she didn't know what they were talking about. And I admit I did this frequently, as a way of passively getting back at her.

One day my mother came by while we were having an argument. I don't remember what it was about—something ridiculous, I'm sure. My mother said, "Give me the baby while you guys talk."

Just then I got a page from the hospital, so I went upstairs to my office to answer the phone. This was in the late eighties when doctors still had beepers. Suddenly the lights went out and I fell to the floor. Chelsea had taken a baseball bat and literally used my skull for batting practice. She knocked me out cold and then immediately ran out of the house, probably frantic because she thought she had killed me.

Shocked to see Chelsea run past her, my mother went upstairs, found me unconscious on the floor, and called an ambulance. They took me to a nearby university hospital, where they ran a bunch of scans and determined that I had a bad cerebral concussion. I did not need surgery, but I could not be left alone because I needed periodic neurological checks.

I had a small amount of bleeding on my brain, and although it wasn't something a CAT scan would pick up—they didn't have MRI technology at that time—they needed to watch out for unconsciousness, lethargy, and other typical signs of problems. So I stayed at my mother's house for several days.

Meanwhile Chelsea was nowhere to be found, so my mother urged me to file a report with the police. At first, I was in no condition to do so, but eventually I went down to the local precinct. To my surprise, Chelsea had filed a complaint! I have no idea what it said, and the police weren't taking it seriously since it was obviously fraudulent. She had assaulted me and then had the audacity to paint herself as the victim! This would become a recurring theme in our relationship.

Chelsea eventually came back to the house, while I was asleep, and spoke with my mother. I don't know what they discussed, but from my mother's point of view, Chelsea had calmed down. However, I was still livid. My wife was psychotic, and I didn't know what to do about it. I couldn't leave her, because that meant leaving my son alone with her, so the marriage continued.

Even with Chelsea's outbursts of rage, the early years of marriage were okay. I realized that something significant was missing, but I was an old-fashioned Italian guy. I told myself, *I've made a mistake, but I'm married and I gotta live with my mistake.* So I kept plugging away, working hard to support her and the kids.

In 1990, I had an opportunity to relocate to Kissimmee, Florida. I flew down with my wife and son, and we stayed at a nice hotel near the urology practice. After my interview, we planned to visit Disney World. The interview went well and I was offered a position as a partner, so I went back to our hotel and told my wife the good news.

I felt like I was coming down with something, and then it suddenly hit me like a ton of bricks. I was running a high fever with aches and pains, sweats, nausea, and vomiting. The bed became drenched with my perspiration, and I was extremely dehydrated. I wasn't even able to get out of bed, and Chelsea and my son were nowhere to be found. With no help, I thought I was going to die. They disappeared for several days, and I finally called my parents in New York and told them what was going on.

My father and mother got on the next plane and came straight to my hotel. Miraculously Chelsea and my son showed up just as my father, who had examined me, told me that I had swine flu. He was able to obtain some intravenous fluids and start an IV on me to get my electrolytes back to normal. When I was stabilized, we all packed up and took the same flight back to New York, where I fully recuperated. This incident clearly demonstrates Chelsea's pattern of running away in times of crisis. She was neither a good mother nor a good wife, and I sometimes wonder whether she had wanted the swine flu to kill me.

Things seemed to get worse and worse. After I gave Chelsea a credit card, which had a $25,000 limit, I got a call from the bank that the account was overdrawn. I asked, "What the hell? Did someone steal my card?" Apparently, Chelsea had gone on a shopping spree, buying a lot of things that she didn't need.

After the divorce, I learned from my mother that Chelsea had also gone on shopping sprees of a different kind while we were married—without using the credit card at all. She would go out and shoplift, with my young son in the shopping basket! I guess she was a thrill seeker.

According to my mother, Chelsea had showed up at her house one day and asked, "Mom, you like my new sunglasses?"

My mother had replied that they were very nice—and obviously very expensive, since Gucci is always expensive! "How much did they cost?" she asked.

Obviously boasting, Chelsea had replied, "They didn't cost me a cent. I stole them!"

"How can you go around stealing like that?" my mother had asked.

"It's no big deal," Chelsea had replied. In addition to her other deficiencies, she was a kleptomaniac.

Chelsea had been a drug addict before I met her, and I had thought I'd be able to change her. Before our wedding, she'd promised that she would learn to read and write, earn her GED, and better herself. That was even included in our prenuptial agreement. While we were married, I hired the best tutors and psychologists for her, and I really believed that she was attending tutoring sessions for her dyslexia. I would give her cash and she would leave our home, supposedly to attend her sessions.

This went on for years. I'd come home and ask, "How are things going?" And she'd reply, "Oh, fabulous, blah blah blah."

One day when I got home early from work, Libby, her tutor, called to ask if Chelsea was out of the hospital yet. I exclaimed, "What?"

"Chelsea told me that she was being hospitalized for treatment of a critical illness. I haven't seen her in five months. Is she okay?"

"You haven't seen her for five months?" I repeated. "You're telling me that she hasn't been to see you, and she hasn't paid you any of the money that I've been giving her for your tutoring sessions?"

Libby reiterated that she hadn't seen Chelsea for five months, and that the story had been that Chelsea was sick and going to the hospital.

Naturally, when I approached Chelsea about this and she realized she was caught, she went ballistic, threw a temper tantrum, and left. Again, twenty-four hours passed and she was nowhere to be found. At least that time she didn't hit me—though I was scarred from all the lies I'd discovered.

Eight years after the divorce, I learned that Chelsea had been going to a friend's house to do drugs. Apparently she had smoked pot and used cocaine, methamphetamine, and God knows what else. I was shocked to learn that she also had affairs with three guys and a woman, but it explained a lot—like why we never had sex during the last six or seven years of our marriage.

The bottom line was that in episode after episode, Chelsea would lie, I would catch her, and then she would do it again. She was pathological—and even worse, she was self-destructive and a danger to our son.

One day in 1990 when I had a full day's schedule, the head nurse came to me during surgery and said, "I need to speak to you after this case, Dr. Panvini. It's urgent."

I responded, "Can you give me an idea of what it's about?"

"After the case," she said.

It was obvious that she didn't want to ruin my concentration. So I finished with the patient and then asked what could be so important.

The head nurse said, "Your son is in the hospital, and your house is burning down."

She told me where my son was, and I left immediately. As I frantically drove to my house, I saw the fire engines. Chelsea had apparently put some bottle nipples to boil on the stove and then forgotten about it. When all the water boiled out, it started a fire. My son had been in a chair in the kitchen when this happened, and he was overcome by fumes. They had to keep him overnight in the hospital.

On another occasion in 2004, after we had moved from New York to Indiana, I got cell phone calls from my son and daughter around nine o'clock at night, just as I was getting ready to go into the operating room. Obviously frantic, they said, "Mommy just ran off the road into a ditch. We don't know what to do, and she's unconscious."

I said, "Don't move, I'll be right over." I called the police, ran out of the hospital, after driving on the road where my children described that she ran off the road in the ditch, realizing that the car was not there and drove home, where I found them unattended. Apparently Chelsea had gotten the car out of the ditch and driven home. But she was so high from whatever drugs she had taken that she had passed out in our bed, leaving the children alone downstairs.

Chelsea was a danger to herself and others, me and our children in particular, and it's amazing that I escaped the marriage alive.

CHAPTER TWELVE

911

As long as I live, I will never forget the events of September 11, 2001. What happened that day had a profound effect on my life in the years that followed, and you could say it was the spark for everything that came afterward, right up to the present day.

I was working at several hospitals in New York at that time, including Saint Vincent's in Manhattan, where I was on call that day. The night before, on September 10, I had dinner with a pharmaceutical company representative at Windows on the World, the restaurant at the top of the World Trade Center's North Tower. My colleagues and I had the last dinner there, literally. I had planned to stay overnight in the city, but I changed my mind and left earlier than I had originally intended because I had patients the next day.

I went home, went to bed, and woke up the next morning at seven. Just as I got in my car, I got a call from the hospital telling me that I had been bumped for an appendectomy, so my first operation would be a couple of hours later than I had planned. I said, "All right," and sat down to watch CNN.

As I was watching the stock market report, the news anchor said there had just been an explosion reported at the World Trade Center. I called out, "Chelsea, come over here. This is where I was last night, and there was an explosion." In those first few moments, they hadn't been sure whether it was a plane or something else.

I was wary about the exponential growth of Muslim population where my Office was located. The whole episode, immediately fostered a lot of questions began going through my mind. Were we under attack, or was this a bizarre accident? I had noticed that in Long Island City, where I had one of my offices, the population had become predominantly Muslim almost overnight.

I was still thinking about that when the second plane hit the other tower. When that happened, I turned to Chelsea and said, "Get in the car. We're under attack, and we have to pick up the children."

Naturally she dismissed my concerns and said, "You're crazy and paranoid."

I said, "Don't argue with me. Just get in the car, and let's get our children from school."

My son and daughter attended schools close to our house. First Chelsea and I picked up our daughter, Natasha, and there were no other parents at that school yet. By the time we picked up my son, though, cars were lined up. Outside the building were police, FBI agents, and crowds of children talking on cell phones to their parents at the World Trade Center.

As we were driving to Vincenzo's school, we heard about Flight 93 going down in Pennsylvania, a thwarted hijacking attempt in Texas, and another plane striking the Pentagon. I could see the frightened look on Chelsea's face as she realized that this was a reality and said, "Oh my God, are we really under attack?"

When we arrived at Vincenzo's school, she frantically ran inside to get him. I stayed in the car, with Natasha in the back seat. It was a bright sunny day, but the gloom of catastrophe had started to affect every New Yorker with memories that will never be forgotten.

While waiting for Chelsea, I watched the FBI agents and the poor children crying as they talked to their parents. In the distance, I could see plumes of smoke coming from the World Trade Center. The situation was surreal, and as I think of it today, I still get chills. So many people were affected, including the children right there in front of me. I watched them with tears in their eyes, yelling and screaming as they realized that they'd never see their loved ones again. The FBI agents, police officers, school counselors, and teachers were all trying to console the children, while still being puzzled by the attack itself. Our whole world had been fractured, and hearts were bleeding from irreparable damage to the future of all New Yorkers.

As I continued listening to the news in the car, I watched those poor children—just teenagers—sobbing as they talked on their phones and watched the smoke plume in the distance. I could see the plume suddenly get much larger, and then the radio news reporter said, "Ladies and gentlemen, you're not going to believe this, but Tower Two is going down at 9:59 a.m." Suddenly everything went silent for a moment, and then the children began to frantically yell and scream, smashing their phones on the ground and punching their fists into the concrete, causing their hands to bleed.

Meanwhile Chelsea found Vincenzo inside the school building and brought him outside. As she was putting him in the car, the reporter said, "Ladies and gentlemen, Tower One just came down at 10:28."

None of us said anything as I drove my family home. Then I told them to lock the doors and not answer them for any reason, not waste electricity, and be safe. I had to go into the city because I would be on trauma call to triage patients at Flushing Hospital Medical Center, where I was on staff. Staff surgeons at New York City hospitals are required to respond to any disaster and I had been beeped, so I needed to get to the hospital as soon as possible.

We needed to free up beds for the waves of injured people we assumed would soon be arriving at the hospital. So I had to go through the charts for any patients who didn't desperately need to be there, write prescriptions as needed, and discharge them. After that was done, I went down to the emergency room and waited ... and waited ... and waited. A couple of patients showed up with lung injuries from inhalation of debris, but no survivors from inside the towers themselves.

The next day, after spending the whole night in the hospital, I decided that to truly be of help, I needed to get closer to Ground Zero. So after spending all day at Flushing Hospital, I took it upon myself to go down to the World Trade Center. On a normal day in New York, driving in traffic is a nightmare, but on September 12, the city was virtually paralyzed and everyone was paranoid. It took more than a half hour to drive one mile, because of all the police barricades, security checks, and everything else going on.

When I got to the Fifty-Ninth Street Bridge on September 12, I could see people walking like zombies, covered in what looked like moon dust with glazed looks in their eyes. They were walking along the side of the bridge without any expression of emotion, but tears were carving paths through the soot that was hardening into mud on their faces.

On the other side of the bridge, I saw people directing traffic and stumbling around. Every time I think about it, I get goose bumps. The traffic was horrible, but I spotted a police officer in the middle of the chaos. Wearing my white lab coat, scrubs, and hospital badge, I approached him.

He was directing traffic as best he could, saying, "You can't go here," "You can't go there," and just trying to get people out of the way.

Showing him my badge, I said, "I gotta get down to Ground Zero."

He came up to my car window, ready to dismiss me like everyone else, and said, "You can't go there." But then he looked at me again and said, "Doc?" It just so happened that he was one of my patients. He asked me, "What are you doing here?"

I said, "I work at Saint Vincent's, and I gotta get down to the site to help out."

He motioned as if to say, "Give me your keys."

I looked at him, confused, and asked, "What do you mean?"

He said, "Gimme your keys. I'll show you how to get down there, and I'll take care of your car."

I gave him my keys, got out of the vehicle, and walked down to the site, where the destruction was indescribable. At first I could still see colors, but gradually everything turned more and more gray until at last there was no color whatsoever. I was walking on what looked like moon dust, surrounded by a horrible, acrid smell that was nauseating. To this day, I can still smell that burning flesh, or rubber, or whatever was making that horrible smell.

As I walked along, I could see family photos and other items from people's offices, all of it smashed among the rubble. Sometimes as I kicked the rubble, the moon dust would disperse to reveal soft, unidentifiable things—which I would suddenly realize were parts of human bodies. I continued walking along in horror, as we all were at that time, and eventually I got to Ground Zero.

Just as I got there, there was a big cheer. Apparently they had found one of the firefighters who had been lost the day before in the rubble(September 11), and they were able to rescue him. They transported him right over to Saint Vincent's.

The events of September 11, 2001, are etched in my memory forever, and I lost many good friends that day. But I also witnessed displays of human greed and depravity that showed me just how corrupt some people can be.

At that time I lived in Manhasset, Long Island, where a lot of stockbrokers lived. They took the Long Island Railroad into Manhattan every morning to avoid the headaches of driving to work. After the 9/11 disaster, I saw waves of lawyers haunting the parking lot at the train station. They were writing down the license plate numbers of abandoned cars, tracking down the vehicles' owners through DMV records, going to the houses, approaching the widows, and making lowball offers on their houses. Those people were depraved parasites—it was unbelievable. I learned about this from one of my patients who worked at the Department of Motor Vehicles on Long Island.

My office was converted to a triage center for firefighters and police officers. I didn't see my regular patients; if I was able to get to the office, I spent my time there assisting the police and firefighters. I made it to the office maybe twice during that first week, just to help out, but beyond that I was paralyzed.

New York changed on that day. In my mind, the question wasn't *if* but *when* the next attack would occur, and it weighed heavily on me. I grew tired of holding my breath as I went through a tunnel or over a bridge, worrying that the car or truck in front of me was packed with C4 or some other explosive. I no longer felt good about New York, so two years later, I put my house up for sale after a very serious near-death event.

One night after finishing rounds at Mary Immaculate hospital in Jamaica, Queens, I was no more than two miles away from the hospital when I got a stat call from the operating room for a renal trauma with multiple gunshot wounds. I got on the phone with the residents and instructed them how to get control of the bleeding vessels before I arrived.

When I got there, I saw multiple gunshots to the kidney, liver, spleen, and intestines. I did my part, which meant doing a partial nephrectomy and stopping the bleeding by doing a splenectomy, and left the rest to the general surgeons. One of the residents turned to me and said, "You know, this guy is really going to thank you!"

"I'm sure he will," I responded.

"No, I mean he's really going to thank you."

I leaned over the drape sheet, saying, "Who are we operating on, the president?" It turned out to be one of my surgical colleagues. He had been in the same parking lot I had just left when he'd gotten caught in the crossfire from a gang fight. The realization that that could've been me on that operating room table woke me up to the point where I decided living in New York was hazardous to your health. The next week I decided to leave New York.

CHAPTER THIRTEEN

The Indiana Debacle

When I decided to leave New York, I didn't have a plan in mind. I simply came home one day with a map of the United States, taped it up in our living room, and asked Chelsea, Vincenzo, and Natasha to throw a dart at it. Wherever the dart landed, that was where we'd be moving. Right away my daughter threw a dart that landed in the middle of Indiana, so that's where we moved—to a cornfield in Indiana.

I was able to sell the house for a good profit, and we packed up as I closed my practice in the city. I immediately found a job in Indiana that paid me handsomely, and I was able to get my state medical license within six weeks. We took trips to look for a house and eventually found one that was newly built but still needed some work. The entire transition took approximately three months, and then I started a practice in Indiana.

Moving was not a decision that Chelsea supported. She told me, "I can't believe you moved us from New York to this piece of shit place. I can't stand it here." She was not at all happy about moving to Indiana, although it was the best thing for the children.

One night not long after we got there, I was walking outside with my daughter, and she asked, "Daddy, what are those white things up in the sky?"

I asked, "What white things? Are you talking about the stars? The moon?"

She didn't know what to call them, but she was pointing to the stars. Then it dawned on me that she'd never seen stars in New York because of all the light pollution. Indiana was a whole new world for my children. For the first time, they were able to ride bikes and do lots of other fun childhood things. It really seemed like the best thing for everyone, and our lives were on a path to peace and tranquility. Of course, Chelsea had to find a way to blow it all up.

When we lived in New York, Chelsea suffered from a condition called Ramsay Hunt syndrome (herpes zoster of the trigeminal nerve), which affects the facial nerves near one ear. She would have painful attacks of Bell's palsy, a paralysis of the face, almost weekly. In New York, probably because of her dyslexia, she had been cautious about venturing into new neighborhoods or going to unfamiliar locations, because she didn't want to get lost. The stress of her dyslexia and illiteracy, combined with the illness, was creating a lot of issues for her.

I took her to more than twenty pain management and infectious disease specialists to find a way to manage her Ramsay Hunt syndrome, but no one was able to do anything for her. Several procedures were performed on her—stellate ganglion blocks and other things that never seemed to provide her with any relief. She couldn't take narcotics, so she was on another type of medication that carried the risk of kidney damage and organ damage, and she was getting to high levels.

Without my knowledge, Dr. Hastings, at the pain management clinic at Long Island Jewish Medical Center, told Chelsea that it was too bad marijuana wasn't legal, because that would probably be the best thing for her. She hid this conversation from me, just as she hid so many other things.

I later learned that marijuana was used in the 1930s to treat shingles, as well as other types of pain, including PMS. Marijuana has neuro-stabilizing effects and was used for pain control and neuropathy. So, also without my knowledge, Chelsea took a large quantity of marijuana with her from New York to Indiana, where she hid it in boxes in the garage.

One night I said, "Chelsea, it looks like the lack of stress from living in New York seems to be helping you. You're not having episodes as often."

She answered, "It's not the change in the environment."
"What do you attribute it to?" I asked.

"Marijuana."

I couldn't believe it. I was livid. Only then did she tell
me what Dr. Hastings had recommended and how much
marijuana she had brought to Indiana with her.

"Chelsea, this isn't going to work," I said. "You don't know
what that marijuana has been laced with, and you don't know
anything about what you're putting into your body. Yeah, it
may have some effect, but you don't know what causes that
effect."

After my initial anger, I did some research and found
that marijuana was used for pain management in a variety
of circumstances. At that time, in the early 2000s, few states
had legalized it, and I admit that I was very much against it
initially. But then I began to understand some of its medicinal
uses and could see the improvement in Chelsea, who had
been chronically depressed and even suicidal. In fact, she had
been so depressed that I was having to keep guns away from
her and ration her pain medications for fear she might try to
hurt herself.

I had empathy for Chelsea's situation and understood that
there were legitimate issues at play. So I called Dr. Hastings,
with her permission, and spoke to him myself. He explained
why he had made that recommendation, and he gave me

information to look up. I did my research and found that what he said was true.

Then I said to Chelsea, "Look, this state doesn't have legalized marijuana, although apparently some states do. I don't want anything to do with this. You're going to have to figure out some way to do it on your own."

So she did. Sasha, Chelsea's sister, a drug addict and a big pothead, taught my wife how to grow marijuana. Chelsea set up a small area in our basement with a few lights and a lot of plants. She wasn't a green thumb by any means, and none of the plants were more than four or five inches high. The whole thing was ridiculous, and when she told her sister about the trouble she was having, Sasha agreed to send her some seeds by mail.

The seeds that Sasha mailed to Chelsea were not intercepted by the police or the postal authorities, but something that they ordered online from overseas was. So one day when I was working in my office, I got a call from Chelsea.

"Dino, the police are at our house, and they have a search warrant. What should I do?"

I asked, "What's the problem?" I had no idea what was going on with her growing operation, which I hadn't wanted anything to do with. I had warned her, "Look, if it helps you, fine. But stay out of trouble and don't buy things off the street."

On the phone, she told me, "The police, Customs agents, and the postmaster general are here. They want the key to the basement."

"You have the key, Chelsea."

"No, I don't."

"Chelsea, you go down to the basement every day."

She insisted that she didn't have the key. If I had known then what I know now—about all the ways she would attempt to destroy my life in the years to come—I would've immediately realized that she was attempting to incriminate me by branding me as a participant in her criminal activities. But I was still innocent in many ways.

I told her I would be right home. As soon as I arrived, I began to ask questions of the assembled authorities.

The postmaster told me, "We intercepted a package of seeds ordered in your wife's name. They came from overseas and were intercepted by Customs, and we have a warrant to search the premises."

I told them that they were free to search. Since I didn't know what they would find in the basement, I was somewhat ambivalent, but there really was no other option. I questioned why Chelsea didn't just allow them downstairs herself, but I tried to remain calm, collected, and cordial.

I had been working so hard to establish my practice that I had never taken the time to see what was going on downstairs. But when I got there, accompanied by the police and other authorities, I saw that she had hooked up lights to grow thirty or forty small plants, though none had grown large enough to be harvested.

The next thing I knew, Chelsea and I were both wearing handcuffs. I protested, saying, "What the hell's going on here? I had nothing to do with this. I didn't even know anything about it."

They said, "It's in your house, and the house is in your name." And that's how I was dragged into Chelsea's chaos once again.

I had patients to see the next day, and by then the entire town knew what had happened. Competitors in town who didn't like me made sure the news was broadcast widely—local newspapers, television, radio, and the internet—and that my reputation was completely tarnished. One article said, "Dr. and wife arrested for marijuana growing operation in their home. Thirty plants confiscated by police. Dr. Panvini's license is suspended by Indiana medical licensing board."

I had to hire an attorney and was forced to plead guilty to a misdemeanor, though eventually I had it expunged. I don't know if Chelsea did the same, and I don't care. That long, drawn-out battle destroyed my career in Indiana and left a major blemish on my medical license.

The Indiana medical licensing board falsely accused me of treating my wife with medical marijuana. They threatened me, saying, "If you don't plead guilty, we'll have your license revoked forever." This was a lie, but they had to come up with something or they'd look foolish—which they did.

I fought it as hard as I could. I had testimonials from patients, doctors, and friends—hundreds of people telling the medical licensing board what a good doctor I was and that I had never been impaired. They performed hair, urine, and blood analyses on me, and everything came back negative. When they performed the same tests on Chelsea, everything came back positive—for obvious reasons.

The medical board had put a summary suspension on my license the moment I was charged, so now they had egg on their faces. They had to make something stick to make themselves look good, so they demanded that I plead guilty to treating Chelsea. Naturally I protested, but they said, "Well, then you're going to lose your license."

My lawyer, Matthew Wiley, was a tall, fat, arrogant man with gray hair. Also, money hungry, he was the most famous attorney in Indiana because he took care of many important celebrities, including the NASCAR drivers. Wiley told me, "Look, just take the deal."

In retrospect, I should have fought harder, but I was dealing with a bunch of redneck idiots who couldn't admit that they'd made a mistake and a corrupt lawyer who just wanted to end the case regardless of the repercussions for me. They knew that I hadn't been treating Chelsea, because I presented them with exhaustive documentation that she was being treated by Dr. Hastings and more than twenty other specialists around the country. I gave them evidence of her health problems and the fact that her symptoms were improving.

I later found out that my lawyer was padding his bill by reporting me to the Drug Enforcement Administration (DEA). The DEA sent me a notice that I had to sign an agreement stating that I would never again treat a patient with medical marijuana—which I never had!

But I had learned about the research being done on medical marijuana in treating patients for things such as interstitial cystitis and chronic neuropathy, and I knew that signing that agreement would prevent me from keeping abreast of future advances in my field. So, I refused to sign that sloppy agreement, because the federal government was simply behind the times. Numerous research studies had shown positive results and promised clinical benefits for patients suffering from, for example, chronic pain and seizure disorders.

Then things really started to go south. I began overhearing phone conversations between Chelsea and her sister about ways to put the blame on me, which was absurd to even contemplate. I had negative blood toxicology, hair analysis, and urinalysis reports, while she had positive results—and she wanted to blame me? It was completely irrational.

Emotionally I was at the lowest point of my entire life. I questioned God and asked why he would allow such a thing to happen to me at the peak of my career, even though I knew that's not how God works. I was depressed and confused about what the future had in store for me. I asked for advice from some friends in New York, including previous patients who were lawyers.

To get my mind off my problems, I enrolled in the University of Phoenix's online MBA program and took some business courses. Since I couldn't practice medicine at the time, I thought that would strengthen some areas of deficiency in my education.

When I overheard the conversations between my wife and her sister, I began to feel less certain about the future of my marriage. Fortunately, a way out presented itself. I was working at one of the local hospitals, and the management there said, "Listen, we don't care what the newspapers say. You're more than welcome to operate in our facilities here. You do good work." So I concentrated my efforts there.

Then an opportunity emerged in Washoe County, Nevada, in a small city near Reno, and I decided to move there. As I was packing and getting ready to leave Indiana by myself, since the children were in the middle of the school year, Chelsea asked, "Why don't you tell me that you love me anymore?"

I turned to face her and said, "Because I don't."

How could I love someone who had nearly destroyed my career? Someone who had attacked me in so many ways—mentally, emotionally, and even physically? I had no idea that the worst was yet to come.

CHAPTER FOURTEEN

Attempted Murder by Wife

Chelsea filed for divorce on Christmas Eve, December 24, 2006. On the previous day, she had paid her lawyer $50,000 using one of my credit cards. As bad as things were between us, some part of me was still the loyal husband. I was trying to keep our family together and make our marriage work, despite being repeatedly confronted with her lies, rage, negligent parenting, and all the rest.

She would lie about the smallest, pettiest things. One evening, while we were still living in New York, she must have been irritated by my comments about her never cooking and constantly taking the children to McDonald's and Burger King to eat. When I came home from work, a lavish meal was laid out in the kitchen.

I said, "Wow, Chelsea, what happened here?"

"I've been cooking all day for you," she said.

I was genuinely surprised. "You cooked?"

"Yeah," she said, "your mother told me what to do."

I told her that I was impressed—and part of me really was. She had prepared spaghetti, meatballs, and a full Italian dinner. I said, "Let me go wash up, and then we'll eat." But as I glanced at the trash can on my way out of the room, I saw that she had ordered the food from some pizza parlor down the street.

Deciding not to make anything of it, I cleaned myself up, came back downstairs, and asked again, "Wow, you cooked all this yourself?"

"Yes, every bit of it." She was a pathological liar, and she simply refused to drop her story.

I didn't mention it again until after dinner, when I said with a smile, "Chelsea, you'd better throw away the evidence from the trash bin."

She was livid and instantly threw one of the temper tantrums with which I was already deeply familiar. But at least that time she didn't hit me.

By 2006, things had gotten really bad. I had moved to the Reno area in the wake of the marijuana scandal in Indiana, and I was working in Washoe County, Nevada. But I was still hoping that we could be a family and make things work, so

I was getting ready to bring Chelsea and the kids to Nevada permanently.

I had picked out a beautiful house with a big backyard, and it was in a neighborhood with great schools. I brought them all there so they could explore the place and get used to the idea of living in Nevada, which after all is quite different from Indiana. Just going from cornfields to the desert would be a major transition for a child, but I was sure they would like it.

I was right. Vincenzo and Natasha loved the house, and they were perfectly happy, even excited, about moving. But Chelsea hated the house, though I have no idea why. She didn't even attempt to make a rational argument; it was like she was acting out of pure spite.

"There's no goddamn way you're going to move me to the middle of the desert. I hate this house! Why did we ever leave New York?" She did everything short of stamping her feet.

"Well, it'll have to do for the time being," I said. "Prices are high around here, unless you want to just rent a place."

She stuck to her guns, saying, "I don't like the house. There's nothing to like about it."

The children were running around somewhere outside as we had this argument alone in the kitchen. I was sitting on the floor with my back against the wall.

Without warning, she flew into a rage. She was wearing cowboy boots, and before I could react, she kicked me in the balls so hard that I still suffer from the injury today. The woman was becoming a threat to my very life. If I didn't wind up in jail because of her, I might well have found myself in the hospital—or the morgue.

I spent most of 2006 living alone, because Chelsea and the children never moved to Nevada. As it turned out, that was fortunate for them. No sooner had I made the down payment than the house began to be regularly shaken by violent earthquakes. Apparently the epicenter was right underneath my new house! I was forced to leave, but I was able to get the down payment refunded. I later learned that the house was eventually swallowed up by the earth.

Later that year, I needed to return to Indiana to take care of some issues with the state medical board. So I decided that I would surprise Chelsea and visit without telling her I was coming.

I was in my office in Sparks, seeing the day's patients, when I received a phone call. My secretary said, "There's a police officer who needs to speak with you. He says it's urgent."

I went in my office, sat down at my desk, and picked up the phone. The man on the other end said, "Dr. Panvini? This is Sergeant Ernest Smith of the Bartholomew County sheriff's department in Indiana. We have reason to believe that your life is in danger."

At first, I thought it was one of my friends playing a prank. I laughed and said, "All right, Doug, nice try. Try another one."

But the man was insistent. "No, sir, this really is Sergeant Ernest Smith from the Bartholomew County sheriff's department. We have reason to believe that your wife is planning to assassinate you."

"Are you kidding me? Who is this really?" I still couldn't believe what I was hearing.

He repeated himself a third time, and then he began probing a bit. "Listen, you're coming to Indiana soon, are you not?"

I asked, "How do you know that?"

"Well, sir, your wife knows that you're coming. We strongly recommend that you *not* go home during your visit, because your wife has been planning to assassinate you. She has been asking about the ramifications if she accidentally shoots her husband when he walks into her house without her prior knowledge. Apparently she has asked people she knows in the local courthouse downtown about the ramifications of an accidental murder and whether she would be prosecuted if it was an accident."

As I listened to Sergeant Smith, I couldn't believe what I was hearing and what an idiot she was! I'm sure she had gotten answers that kept her from actually trying anything; so-called "stand your ground" and home-invasion self-defense laws weren't as common then as they are now. Still, that's what the officer told me. And she had apparently asked those questions of several people!

I was astonished, flabbergasted, stunned. I would've been in mortal danger. What could I do about something like this? I didn't know what to say to the officer, so I thanked him for letting me know and hung up.

Obviously, my plan to surprise my wife and children went out the window. I was still required to go to Indiana to take care of things with the state medical board, but I kept my movements a secret.

Still, while I was in Indiana, I got a call from my daughter, Natasha, who was fourteen years old. She asked, "Daddy, why aren't you coming home?"

I said, "Natasha, I'm at work." I didn't want to tell her that I was in Indiana. I had to deceive my own daughter to protect myself from my insane wife! I told her that I had a lot of patients and was very busy.

But Natasha insisted, "No, you're in Indianapolis."

"Natasha, who told you that?" The answer was obvious, of course. Chelsea had told her where I was. She had the whole thing planned out. Had the Bartholomew County sheriff not called me, you wouldn't be reading this right now.

Then I told my daughter, "Put your mother on the phone." When Chelsea picked up, I said, "What are you telling our kids?"

Chelsea said, "I'm telling them that you're in Indiana."

"No, I'm not." I lied to her, too, because I had no choice. I didn't want her to find out where I was, for fear that she would hunt me down and shoot me.

There was an arsenal of guns at the house in Indiana, and most of them were hers. Her brother-in-law was a gun dealer in Nebraska, and she had purchased several guns when she lived in the Midwest. In New York they were illegal, so we had kept them in storage when we lived there. But obviously when we moved to Indiana, she had found the boxes in which they were stored.

I never again returned to the Indiana house, and Chelsea soon filed for divorce. But first she emptied my bank accounts, of course, and paid her lawyer, Veronica Fischer, $50,000 with my credit cards.

Later, when Chelsea's attempts to destroy my life got out of control, my father attempted to intercede. He offered her a one-time settlement of a million dollars just to get her to disappear from our lives. She refused. By then it was about hatred and revenge for all the things she believed, in her madness, that I had done to her.

Even today, she continues to pursue me. As I write these words, I have received a notice from the Midwest, where she resides today. She has managed to reopen a case that I thought had been closed while I was comatose in Florida. Apparently, my former attorney did not properly file the paperwork that would have reduced my child support payments during the time while I was living in Italy and not working.

My child support payments during that time went directly to her, rather than through the child support system. I was subject to a court order that required me to contact them at a particular phone number, but the system was down, leaving me with no option but to send checks directly to Chelsea.

Now she has fraudulently asserted that those checks were not child support payments, but personal gifts! As though I would give this demonic woman a dime of my own free will! While I was unconscious and on the brink of death, she was able to convince a court that I owed her more than $67,000 in delinquent child support. If I don't pay, the consequences could be severe. The document reads as follows:

> The support payment records indicate that your court ordered support payments are past due in the amount of $67,000. Under administrative

offset, certain federal payments which might otherwise be paid to you will be intercepted, either in whole or in part, to pay past due child-support. Under federal law and state law, any federal or state tax refund to which you may be entitled may be intercepted and, if so will be used to satisfy your debt.

Your debt will remain subject to federal tax refund offset, administrative offset, passport certification, and/or state revenue tax offset until it is paid in full. The United States Secretary of State will refuse to issue a passport to you, and will revoke, restrict or limit a passport which was previously issued. The amount of your past due will also be reported to the consumer credit reporting agencies.

In addition you will be submitted to authorized federal agencies and lending institutions that offer federal loans, loan guarantees and loan insurance. As part of the loan application review process federal agencies are required to deny loans or loan guarantees to individuals who owe delinquent support. Additionally you will be reported to any state or federal licensing agencies to restrict any of your licenses including driver's license.

So my passport, medical license, and driver's license would be revoked, and my bank accounts would be frozen or seized. She would be able to completely destroy me once and for all, as she has wanted to do every day since Christmas Eve of 2006. Fortunately, the issue has since been resolved. But as you can see, she remains relentless—even after twelve years.

CHAPTER FIFTEEN

The Nevada Rues

My wife had filed for divorce, stolen my money, and effectively taken my children away from me and poisoned them against me. It would take more than a decade to rebuild my relationship with my daughter, Natasha, and my relationship with my son, Vincenzo, has never been the same. I was literally alone in the desert, living in Nevada in 2007 with no one to support me through these traumas or help me keep my life on track.

Fortunately, my professional career was going well. I was working in Sparks with a full roster of patients whose care was entirely in my hands. I was doing the best work I could for everyone who came through my operating room and achieving great results. No matter what else was going on in my life, at least no one could say I was not a talented and hardworking physician who cared for the people who sought my help. That was the one thing no one could take away from me.

Or so I thought.

One day I was on call at the hospital with a full load of patients for the day. Then the head nurse notified me that I needed to report to administration as soon as I finished the case I was working on in the operating room. I had no idea what could possibly be happening. Everything had been going fine, and I hadn't heard about any dissatisfied patients filing malpractice complaints or anything like that.

As requested, I went upstairs to the administrative offices, where I was shocked at what I found. Everyone had grim looks on their faces, and some avoided making eye contact with me.

I tried to lighten the mood. "What's up?" I asked. "Who died?"

No one laughed, and their grim expressions didn't change.

One hospital administrator said to me, "Dr. Panvini, you need to surrender your ID badge. You are summarily suspended and forbidden from entering the hospital or providing care to our patients."

I couldn't believe what I was hearing. There hadn't been a single complaint about my work! Letting my temper get the better of me, I asked, "What the fuck is going on here?"

The administrator said, "We have reason to believe that you're a drug addict."

Now I was really angry. "Who the hell said that?" I demanded. But a moment later, it became clear to me. "Wait a minute. This is coming from my ex-wife, isn't it?"

There was no way it could be anyone but Chelsea. She knew that since the pot affair, there was a chance that people would believe this kind of outlandish and fraudulent accusation against me. It was the perfect weapon in her attempt to destroy me.

The administrator tried to deny that Chelsea was the source of the false accusation. "Legally, we cannot reveal the source," he said. "That's hospital protocol."

I'm sure that Chelsea knew that her identity would be kept secret, probably because Veronica Fischer had told her. Still, the body language in that office gave her away. The moment I said her name, the administrators' pupils dilated and their posture shifted. There was no way it could have been anyone else.

I had to surrender my badge and leave the facility immediately, abandoning all the patients who had come to see me. Just like in Indiana, I had to undergo in-depth drug testing. They performed a urinalysis, blood analysis, and hair analysis, and it took two weeks for the results to come back. During that time, I had no option but to sit at home, earning no money and helping no patients, waiting to be proven innocent of Chelsea's false and frankly libelous charges.

Finally the test results arrived, and of course they were negative. I returned to the hospital enraged by the way everyone there had treated me. I demanded that they make a formal apology, but ultimately I was too disgusted by their behavior to continue working for such people. A member of the Hospital Corporation of America, no less!

I said to the administrators, "Look, you'd better find a new urologist, because I'm not going to be put through anything like this again. I have a psychopathic ex-wife who will do anything to destroy me, and you played right into her hands. You need to know that what you have done here is horrible."

The worst part about it was that the story spread beyond the hospital. Once again, my name was being poisoned in a community where I had few friends or connections. Someone—or several people—in the hospital administration had loose lips, and suddenly everyone in Sparks seemed to know that the new urologist had been accused of being a drug addict.

Chelsea would employ this tactic again and again. Her false legal charges would somehow become the subject of gossip around town, no matter where I went. She followed me like a black cloud, raining her hatred down on me with the help of her lawyers and the court system, which they always manipulated in her favor.

As if my professional troubles weren't enough, before I could leave Nevada, I was struck with a medical emergency. One day, as I was winding down my practice in Sparks, I was moving a patient from the operating room table to a gurney. Without warning, my legs lost all feeling and collapsed beneath me. I fell to the floor, physically paralyzed and in a terrified shock.

I was rushed to a different hospital, one with a neurosurgeon on staff. Paralyzed from the waist down, I was given a diagnosis of cauda equina syndrome with spinal cord stenosis. To regain the use of my legs, I required a complete spinal cord reconstruction complete with screws, rods, and cages.

My recovery took six months. When I finally got back on my feet, I said to myself, *There's something wrong here. Nevada is not for me.* Between the earthquakes, fires, floods, drug charges, and paralysis ... Well, it was time to move on. I let my staff go, shut down my office, and looked for a place in Las Vegas to store my professional materials and records while I decided on my next step.

CHAPTER SIXTEEN

The Divorce

Returning to work at the hospital in Washoe County, Nevada, was difficult. I had been the subject of a malicious and humiliating attack on my professional and personal reputation when my ex-wife accused me of being a drug addict. The medical executive committee and hospital administration had treated me like a criminal, and I had been escorted off the grounds by security. They had another doctor treat my patients so that there would be no problems, but how was I to know whether that doctor would treat them as well as I would have? The baseless campaign against me might have put my patients at risk!

Naturally I had been proven innocent. Throughout our entire lives together—and, I assumed, now that we were divorced and living apart—Chelsea had been heavily involved in drugs. In contrast, I barely even drank alcohol; at most, I had a glass of wine with dinner.

As a physician, I'm keenly aware of the effects of drugs on the body and particularly the damage they can do to the internal organs over time. The liver and kidneys take a real beating from heavy drug use; in many cases, they simply lose the ability to pump toxins out of people's systems at the rate they're putting them in. So I have always stayed away from drugs. But the hospital that employed me, and which I had assumed would support me, turned on me based on nothing but the word of a paranoid, hostile, vindictive drug user—and they wouldn't even admit it!

Once the truth came out, of course, they allowed me to return to work, acting like they were doing me a favor rather than covering up their own mistake. But the damage was done. For one thing, I wasn't in a position to take a financial blow like that. Chelsea had left me penniless after the divorce, so being out of work, even for a few weeks, was tough.

The real problem, though, was the damage to my reputation. Once a story like that gets out, especially in a small place, there's no going back—and we're talking about a town with a population of just over ninety thousand. The word had gone out that I was a drug addict, so by the time I got back to work, I might as well have showed up with a needle hanging out of my arm.

Being proven innocent by the blood, urine, and hair analyses had almost no effect on how I was perceived, when compared with the effect of the initial accusation. And naturally the hospital didn't want me to talk about the case and try to regain my good name. They just wanted me to get back to work and deliver the high-quality care for which they'd hired me in the first place.

As the old saying goes, a lie can travel halfway around the world while the truth is putting its shoes on. In most cases, an accusation is all that's necessary for damage to be done. There's a famous story of a politician who told one of his speechwriters to level a disgusting allegation against one of his opponents. When told that the accusation was obviously untrue, the politician replied that he knew that, but he wanted to force his opponent to deny it.

This has been one of Chelsea's primary tactics ever since she first filed for divorce. Without a shred of proof, she has repeatedly accused me of all sorts of terrible things. Even when the courts strike her down, she comes back with another version of the same story—or some new charge that I have to devote time and money to refute. Furthermore, the penalties she attempts to extract would be unreasonable even if her accusations were true.

What's even more bizarre is the way she's able to manipulate the system. When we were working out our divorce settlement, I hired forensic accountants to go through every penny of our finances. I had volumes of testimony describing exactly where the money was coming from and where it was going. Her attorney, Veronica Fischer, came into the meeting with numbers on a napkin. And the judge accepted her version of finances owed and gave Chelsea everything she asked for.

Chelsea left our marriage with millions of dollars, effectively draining my bank accounts, forcing me to pay her legal fees and buy her a new house, and demanding child support on top of it all. There was absolutely nothing fair or impartial about that settlement. The judge must have been influenced in some way, financially or otherwise; I find it impossible to arrive at any other explanation.

That was not a typical divorce. In her original divorce plea, filed by Veronica Fischer, Chelsea claimed that I had attempted to murder her. I was told that I needed a criminal lawyer, so I hired one, but that ultimately proved unnecessary. She dropped those charges after my attorney challenged her, because she was in violation of Trial Rule 11. When an attorney brings certain allegations to court, they must have indisputable evidence to support those allegations. Obviously, they had no evidence because the attempted murder had never happened. I had never needed a criminal attorney, but she wanted to make the divorce a three-ring circus any way she could.

Stories told by a pathological liar are usually related to something devious that the person herself has done. In this case, Chelsea was accusing me of attempted murder while she was trying to kill me, as I had been warned by the Bartholomew County Sheriff's Department.

For all her intellectual and educational deficiencies, Chelsea was extremely devious and a skilled liar. She was born and raised Catholic, like me, but in Indiana she began attending a Protestant church. Most people in town were members of that denomination, and she used the church for personal gain in an extremely manipulative fashion.

During the divorce trial, as she was giving her testimony under oath to the judge, she made up a story to gain his sympathy. She had brought the members of her Protestant church with her, with the intent of using them as witnesses during the divorce proceedings. They packed the entire courtroom and the corridor outside as well. When I saw this, I wondered what she had up her sleeve.

Chelsea testified that I threatened her life every time I didn't get my way, which was preposterous; never in my life have I attempted to harm anyone. With her church friends watching, she testified that I would threaten to shoot her! She was holding a small drawstring purse that held a bullet wrapped in a swatch of red cloth. She carefully took the bullet out, pressed it to her forehead, and testified under oath that her life had been in danger. According to her, I would hold that bullet to her forehead and say, "If you don't do what I want you to do, I will shoot you."

Unfortunately for her, Chelsea was not a very good liar at that time, and her church friends realized exactly what she was doing. One by one, they got up and walked out of the courtroom. It was obvious that they were disenchanted with hearing Chelsea lie under oath, and not one of her alleged witnesses was willing to testify. Even the judge rolled his eyes as he listened to her, so my attorney and I saw that he knew she was lying. She looked like a fool. I asked my attorney, Mr. Young, to file perjury charges, but he didn't think that was necessary.

Chelsea had also brought one of her other sisters, Tanya Vaughn, as a witness. Tanya started her testimony with nonsensical statements, asserting that Chelsea had told her that I was an evil man and that I would threaten her. There wasn't much substance to any of it, and it fell apart quickly when my lawyer cross-examined her.

"Did Dr. Panvini ever treat you in an evil fashion?"

"Never," she answered.

"Did Dr. Panvini ever treat your sons or your husband or yourself in a negative fashion?"

Again she answered, "No, never."

"Did Dr. Panvini ever treat your son, Bruno, in a negative fashion?"

At that point, Tanya broke down and cried. When Bruno had been a young boy, their family physician had treated a bump on his forehead by prescribing ice packs. I had been finishing my urological residency, and Tanya had asked me for a second opinion.

When I examined Bruno, I found the bump, on his forehead above the bridge of his nose, but I didn't think it was the result of a trauma. I said to his mother, "This doesn't look right. I really would like Bruno to have a CAT scan and some X-rays." The results showed a tumor that was potentially malignant, so I told Bruno and Tanya that he needed to be seen by an ear, nose, and throat specialist as soon as possible. Then I set them up with a reputable physician, who said the tumor should be considered malignant until proven otherwise and recommended surgery.

When they operated on Bruno, they took biopsies and went through the long, tedious process of dissecting the tumor, which was apparently growing out of his frontal sinus. The surgery took almost all day, and they removed most of the tumor. The pathology had revealed a malignant rhabdomyosarcoma of the frontal sinus, which is at the level of the forehead and invading surrounding areas close to the brain but not penetrating the dura mater, which is basically a capsule around the brain and spinal cord.

The surgeon told Tanya and Bruno that they weren't able to remove the entire cancer. Furthermore, it was a type that grows locally and tends to spread into surrounding tissues, although it didn't appear to have spread to other organs. So Bruno had a confined malignant cancer with some portions still remaining, and he needed additional treatments. Chemotherapy, radiation therapy, and possibly additional surgery were recommended.

That poor child, just sixteen years old, underwent approximately a dozen operations plus chemo and radiation. Eventually his entire frontal sinus, left eye, and part of his cheekbone had to be removed, rendering him permanently disfigured. A mask, called a moulage, was crafted out of silicone to give him the appearance of a normal face, but he still looked like the phantom of the opera.

I had been the family's consulting medical adviser every step of the way, offering guidance and helping them make appropriate decisions. Tragically, ten years later the tumor returned and invaded Bruno's brain. He called to tell me that he had had enough of the surgery and treatments, and he asked me what he could do.

I said, "Bruno, you're the patient. You're the person who's going through this horrendous ordeal. What do *you* want to do?"

"I really can't take this anymore," he answered, "and they're telling me that I'm going to die."

"Bruno, God brought you into my life and me into yours, to extend your life for these precious last ten years," I said. "Granted, life has not been fun with all the surgeries and chemotherapy. But *you* need to make this final decision—not me."

Bruno said, "I really don't want any more treatments."

"Then it seems that you've made your final decision. You realize that without treatment, you'll die, right?" I asked.

Bruno acknowledged that he understood that, but that he couldn't take any more. "I don't want any more treatments. I'd rather die." He didn't last more than a month after making that decision.

So while Tanya Vaughn was on the stand to testify in support of Chelsea, she broke into tears and said, "Dr. Panvini is a fantastic human being. He saved my son's life and gave us ten more years together. I have nothing negative to say about Dr. Panvini. He's a wonderful man and a wonderful doctor who has never treated anyone disrespectfully."

Chelsea and her lawyer lowered their heads in embarrassment, as my lawyer finished his cross-examination and said, "Nothing else, Your Honor."

What Chelsea tried to do with Tanya's testimony was totally fraudulent, and it backfired on them when Tanya began to cry. This just shows how evil Chelsea was, trying to get her own sister to commit perjury for her.

Then I asked Mr. Young, my attorney, if Sergeant Ernest Smith would be available to testify about Chelsea's plans to murder me. He said that it would take another day to set up, the cost would be prohibitive, and he just didn't think it was necessary. I was disappointed in him for that, especially since Smith had agreed to be on standby to testify. To this day, I believe that if he had been called, the outcome of the case would have been different. So much for Indiana lawyers!

About that time (2007), something truly strange and frightening changed my perception of the divorce and its aftermath. I came home from work one day and attempted to turn on my home computer, but there was no response. No lights came on and the fan was silent, so I crawled beneath the desk to take a look. Had it been unplugged somehow? No, it was plugged in. I pressed the power button again, but there was still no response. Finally, I decided to take the computer apart and look inside. Perhaps there was some visible damage that I could show to a repairman, so I unscrewed the case and took it apart.

To my surprise, the tower was empty. There was nothing but empty space and dangling cables where the hard drive would normally sit. I couldn't believe what I was seeing. How was this possible? Someone had obviously broken into my home, knowing I would be at the hospital, and removed the hard drive from my computer.

I immediately suspected that someone connected with Chelsea or her attorneys was behind it. They were obviously trying to obtain information about my life that they could then use to create another spurious, fraudulent charge against me, in their never-ending campaign to ruin my life.

I called the police, and when they arrived, I showed them the inside of the computer. They were as surprised as I was, especially since I had seen no evidence of a break-in. No windows were broken, and no locks seemed to have been tampered with. Whoever had come into my home and removed the hard drive must have been an experienced professional, because there were no fingerprints to be found.

Chelsea's brother, John Gardner, was a police officer in the Las Vegas area at the time, but police never go against each other. It's called the "Blue Code." When the police took my statement and inspected the scene, they could find no way to trace who had done it or how. So they told me that there was little they could do to solve the case—and ultimately, they did nothing at all.

Later, during the discovery phase of the divorce proceedings, a photograph of my hard drive was provided by Veronica Fischer! Obviously Veronica and Chelsea had orchestrated the theft. My attorney showed me the photos and some of the files that were present on the drive, but he never asked them how they got that information.

"Why are you not bringing this up during the trial?" I asked him. "This is theft and breaking and entering."

But he just said, "This is the divorce trial, not a criminal proceeding."

After that incident, I began to feel truly unsafe, even more than when I had learned from the sheriff in Indiana about Chelsea's intention to murder me and call it self-defense. I was convinced that I was being watched, and I suspected that my behavior and activities were being recorded to be used as evidence against me in some future legal action. It was impossible to know whom to trust. Anyone in my personal or professional life could be in the employ of Chelsea, her lawyers, or her brothers. Any mistake I made could be used against me at a moment's notice. I was living in a nightmare.

CHAPTER SEVENTEN

Paralysis

My sudden paralysis, which sent me tumbling to the floor after placing a patient on a gurney, was one of the most terrifying experiences of my life. I had not felt any warning signs that would indicate that I was about to be struck with cauda equina syndrome and spinal cord stenosis. I'd had no back problems or numbness in my legs, no difficulty walking or standing. It literally came out of nowhere, and I still have no real explanation for why it happened.

Fortunately I was rushed to a renowned hospital in Reno, Nevada, where they had an excellent neurosurgeon who had been trained in England. He did a fantastic job on me. He had to reconstruct a large portion of my spine from the lumbar region (the lower back) to the sacrum, the so-called *tailbone*. The procedure required screws, plastic rods, and cages around my damaged vertebrae, thereby fusing a large area of my back into position, but some interesting intraoperative findings created additional difficulties.

The surgeon told me afterward that when they put the screws in my spine, it was like putting them into a sponge. I had severe osteoporosis that created more problems than he had anticipated. Apparently, as a surgeon who spent a lot of time in the operating room, I was not exposed to enough ultraviolet light, which is necessary for the effective conversion of vitamin D3 through the skin. Vitamin D3 allows for the absorption of calcium into the bones, and this deficiency was the cause of my osteoporosis. I guess this is an occupational hazard for surgeons.

This condition caused the operation to take longer than it ordinarily would, and it caused the surgical team great difficulty in placing screws and using plates, in addition to the other hardware. I learned this after the operation, when they put me on medication for the osteoporosis.

There were other complications as well. For preventive reasons, I had been taking aspirin every day, which caused me to bleed extensively during the procedure. The blood loss was so severe that during the post-operative period, they wanted to give me a transfusion, but I refused.

Surprised, the surgeon said, "Dr. Panvini, you're a doctor yourself. You know this isn't a good idea."

I said, "No transfusion. If God wants to take me, he will take me." I had been so shocked by the suddenness of the incident, as well as everything that led up to it, that I was feeling extremely fatalistic. At the same time, I had a strong faith that things would take the course they were destined to take. The decision was not really in my hands; it was up to God.

I was raised in the Catholic Church, and I've retained my faith. It has sustained me in some of the darkest periods of my life, and this was definitely one of them. It felt like one more domino falling in a sequence that began as early as 2002, when Chelsea and the kids and I left New York for Indiana. Life had seemed hopeful and full of promise, only to fall apart with the marijuana charges and Chelsea's psychotic rages, impossible behavior, and unsavory friends. By the time I left and she filed for divorce, things were spiraling downward, getting worse and worse as she and her attorneys seemed intent on pursuing me to the ends of the earth. Still, I was able to persevere because of my strong faith, as well as my belief in my own abilities and my mission to help other people with my surgical skills.

The surgeon honored my wishes and did not give me the blood transfusion. Instead, they used a drug called Hespan, which is used to help circulate red blood cells and keep oxygen flowing throughout one's body. This prevents a condition known as hypovolemia (decreased blood plasma volume) that may occur as a result of serious injury, surgery, severe blood loss, burns, or other trauma. The Hespan did its job, and I recovered well from the procedure.

Once my spinal surgery was complete, I went through several months of rehabilitation and physical therapy, as well as ongoing treatment for my osteoporosis. I wore a body cast that immobilized most of my torso, and I had to exercise my legs and learn how to walk again. It took six months before I was able to return to work. I was counting every penny and living on exhaust fumes, which made my daily life almost unbearable. But I had a job lined up that was going to pay me well, so I stuck it out.

That was a difficult time. Though the pain was severe and even incapacitating at times, I was able to push through by recalling other times when I had been near death but had emerged stronger on the other side.

I remember a trip I took to Playa Blanca, Mexico, in 1975. It was a beautiful morning, and I was sitting on the sand with the sun's rays beating down on me. A gentle breeze cooled me gently, and in the distance I saw some local people on sailboats. I decided to go sailing myself, so I rented a small boat, put my life jacket on, and headed out to sea.

The wind was perfect and took me about fourteen miles offshore. The view was absolutely beautiful as I looked back at the beach and a gorgeous villa on the rocky cliffs overlooking the water. The sea was green near the coastline and dark blue where the water was deeper. The gentle breeze made me want to relax and get a good tan, so I took off my life jacket and lay back on the deck, holding the line for the sail in my right hand and using the jacket as a pillow. I was in heaven, completely at peace on the sea and under the sun. The soft breeze and the sound of the water in the background gently rocked me to sleep.

As the waves in the background washed away my stress, I heard a splash. Turning my head, I saw a school of dolphins playing in the ocean some distance away. I was almost in a dream state, imagining being a millionaire on my yacht with a servant hanging me a glass of champagne as I ate caviar on a Ritz cracker. Was it real or simply an illusion? It was fantastic!

Suddenly a gigantic wave washed over my boat and it began to capsize. Water flooded in and soaked me as my sail started to tip sideways. In a state of panic, I felt my adrenaline surge. Looking to my left, I saw a giant whale just at my bow, but not just any whale. It was a giant black-and-white orca—a killer whale! I tried to keep the boat from capsizing by counterbalancing it and standing up with the rope in both my hands. As I struggled to save myself from drowning, I saw another killer whale jumping out of the water just an arm's length away from me.

I was more frightened than I had ever been in my life! I thought I was going to end up as whale bait. There I was in the middle of the Pacific Ocean, miles from shore, standing on a small sailboat that was close to capsizing, with two killer whales circling in the water. My entire life flashed before my eyes, and I thought about the fact that I had never married or had children. (Oh, if only I had known.) I hadn't yet accomplished my life goals, so I had to snap out of it. I had to get out of that situation alive!

After a long struggle, I finally got control of the boat—and suddenly a third whale leapt across my bow! I started to tack back to shore, moving the sail from one side to another and trying to stay out of waves and remain afloat. The whales kept following me, and my heart was racing at what felt like a thousand beats a minute. I was so scared that my hair was standing on end.

I kept tacking the sail toward shore, hoping one of the gentle Mexican breezes would turn into a real wind. *Please go faster, faster*, I thought. I was fifteen miles from shore and it felt like an eternity. I was terrified that I would never see my family again. I was soaking wet not only from the ocean water but also from the sweat streaming off my head and body from fear and exhaustion.

My hands were tired and bleeding from holding the rope so tightly and pulling it with all my strength, but it never crossed my mind that I was getting rope burns and sunburn. I just wanted to get back to the beach. As I approached the rocks piled up by the shoreline, I could see people lying on the sand. I had made it!

I jumped off the boat, swam to shore, and ran up to the beach. As I started yelling that my boat had been attacked by killer whales, a Mexican with a smile on his face stopped me. He said that they were called killer whales because they kill other whales, not humans.

"You mean these are whale killers?" I asked.

He responded with a nod and a smile.

"But I almost drowned out there!"

Then he explained that they had probably been playing with me, the way dolphins sometimes do.

"I wasn't in danger of being eaten alive?" I asked.

He responded, "No, they play with the boats as if they were toys, but they will not harm you."

I felt like an idiot, and my ignorance had almost given me a heart attack. Well, at least I was still alive. Exhausted, I fell to the sand, closed my eyes, and laughed myself to sleep.

Even though it was the result of my own ignorance, that experience made me realize that there are moments when the only correct response is to do everything possible to survive, while at the same time recognizing that ultimately your life is out of your control. And as I recovered from my spinal injury, I returned to that state of mind. I said to myself, *It's not up to me. I'll do everything possible to get better, and if God wants it to happen, it will happen.* We just need to follow the path that he has outlined for us.

CHAPTER EIGHTEEN

Rocky Mountain High

During the same period that I suffered my paralyzing accident, underwent spinal surgery, and began my physical rehabilitation and therapy, I was also attempting to rebuild my career. I had left Nevada after being so shabbily treated by the hospital in the wake of my ex-wife's false allegation that I was a drug addict. I couldn't trust the administration at that hospital to have my back the next time something came down, and with Chelsea running around loose, there was almost guaranteed to be a next time. Her vindictiveness and hostility had not abated, and each time one of her schemes failed, it made her more determined to hatch another. Chelsea is relentless, but so am I.

When I had my back surgery, I had already asked my employees to help close down my practice. They took care of everything in my absence, putting everything I would need, from office equipment to patient files to surgical supplies, into a storage unit in Las Vegas. I left it entirely in their hands and they were terrific, despite having just lost their own jobs.

My staff was just as appalled by the hospital's actions as I was. To my knowledge, they didn't want to have anything else to do with Northern Medical Center, so they immediately began looking for jobs with other hospitals in the Reno, Nevada, region.

After my surgery, I moved to Arizona. After the fires, floods, earthquakes, and dysfunctional hospital administration in northern Nevada, I wanted to live in a state that didn't have natural disasters and work at a hospital that I could trust. I didn't know where I was going to live, I had no job or immediate prospects, and my ex-wife had done everything in her power—short of killing me—to make it impossible for me to practice medicine in Nevada.

Fortunately, after visiting several hospitals in northeastern Arizona, I found a position at Canyon Meadows Medical Center in Fort Mojave. I joined their team as a urologist, and they provided me with a stipend until I could get on my feet—literally, in this case—and get my practice rolling. I set up an office right next to the hospital and began hiring staff and getting organized. I ended up on staff at both Canyon Meadows and another hospital in the area, Bullhead City Medical Center.

Medical licensing is a complex issue. When you graduate from medical school, you don't automatically get a license.

To be certified by the medical board in the state where you expect to practice, you have to take a special exam, your credentials must be verified, and your past is gone over with a fine-toothed comb. But that's not the end of the matter. To maintain your license, you have to keep up to date by taking continuing medical education (CME) courses every year and earning a minimum number of credits. That's what I was doing in New Orleans just before the accident that began this whole story, taking courses to stay informed about breakthroughs in my specialty as a Diplomate of the American Board of Urology.

Furthermore, when a doctor moves from one state to another, he or she must apply for licensure in the new state. It's not like the legal profession, where someone can just apply without being granted a license in the state to try a case, as Connor Truman, Chelsea's attorney, did. Medical licensure isn't automatic, and frankly I would have had legitimate grounds to be concerned had I been terminated by the hospital in Nevada.

Because I left of my own free will, however, there was no problem in Arizona. I was granted reciprocity; the state's medical board acknowledged that I was properly licensed in Nevada and granted me a license to practice in Arizona. I didn't have to take an exam, though I did have to go through the credentialing procedure, which took several months. I think the fact that Canyon Meadows Medical Center was in desperate need of a urologist at that time helped my case. As a respected institution, they were able to facilitate my case and get things handled as quickly as possible.

Between September, when I suffered my paralysis, and February, when I began practicing medicine at Canyon Meadows, I rented a house in a small town in Clark County, at the southernmost point of Nevada. Although it's right on the Colorado River, it's a desert town and gets extremely hot in the summer, sometimes as much as 130 degrees. Even in the winter the temperature stays in the sixties and seventies, and it hardly ever rains. There are nine hotel/casinos in town, and people come there every year to gamble, enjoy water sports on the river, and attend events.

Although I was undergoing rehabilitation and still had limited mobility because of the cast that covered my torso, I had to get my affairs in order. My former employees had given me all the information about the storage unit where my files and office equipment were being kept. So every day I would drive my small Toyota Camry hybrid the ninety-nine miles from Laughlin to Las Vegas, pick up as much of it as I could, and turn around and head back to put it in my house. You see, I was virtually penniless at that time, so I couldn't even afford movers. I had to do everything by myself.

I had a small Toyota Camry hybrid at the time. As I have said, I was in a cast that immobilized a large portion of my body, but I continued to drive back and forth, back and forth, every day. Bit by bit, I moved the entire contents of my professional life from Las Vegas to Laughlin. I was utterly exhausted, both physically and mentally, but my ex-wife had drained away all of my money, leaving me without the luxury of hiring a moving company until I was able to begin collecting a salary from Canyon Meadows Medical Center.

One day, my exhaustion nearly cost me my life. There's a stretch of road between Las Vegas and Laughlin where the road winds through huge mountains and along cliff edges. On this particular trip, I was so tired that I could hardly keep my eyes open, and I started to fall asleep and veer off the road. If the car had gone off the road to the right, I would have plunged thousands of feet over a cliff, and there's no way I would've survived the impact. Fortunately, I veered to my left, where there normally would have been a divider or a guardrail. Instead I slid straight into a ditch and nearly tore the bottom out of my car in the process.

The tires, wheels, and axles were still in relatively decent shape, but the undercarriage and engine were badly damaged. I was deep in the mountains with no cell phone reception. I sat in the car, thinking about the fact that I had escaped death *again* and wondering what my next move would be. With no cell phone reception, I couldn't summon AAA or even the police, but if I could get out of the ditch and back onto the road, I might be able to make it to civilization.

I had one thing in my favor: the Camry was a hybrid. The fuel system seemed to be badly damaged so the gasoline-driven portion of the engine wouldn't work, but with the battery alone, I was able to start the car and get out of the ditch.

Concerned for my safety and the safety of the vehicle, I was forced to travel at no more than five or ten miles per hour, hugging the shoulder of the road all the way through the mountains to my destination. Running on battery power alone and driving slowly, while still shaking with fear after my latest near-death experience, I finally got to a place where I could make a phone call.

By the time I turned the car off again, it was in even worse shape than it had been immediately after the accident. I called AAA and had them tow it to the nearest Toyota dealer.

When we got there, the mechanic at the dealership said, "It's a goner. There's nothing to salvage here."

I said, "I've got an ex-wife who's going to want some documentation of this." As part of the divorce settlement, Chelsea was entitled to one of my cars, and she had chosen the Camry. I was holding onto my other car, a Chrysler Sebring convertible, with the intention of giving it to my son.

The Toyota dealer prepared a report on the Camry, which I asked them to have notarized and send to me. They did so, and I forwarded it to Chelsea. As I had expected, she flew into a rage, and her lawyers went ballistic as well.

I said, "Look, here's the story. Call them if you don't believe me."

They did just that, and everything I had told them was proven to be true. I suppose they thought I was lying, or that I had destroyed the car on purpose.

I got around town in the Sebring for a while. After I had started work in earnest at Canyon Meadows and had some money to my name again, I bought another Camry hybrid, because that first one had saved my life. Since that day, I've always owned hybrids.

CHAPTER NINETEEN

Parental Alienation

Anyone who has been through a divorce that involves children is probably familiar with the term *parental alienation*, and those who aren't should count themselves lucky. There's a professional history documenting this phenomenon back to the 1980s, though it was first described in 1976 as *pathological alignment*.

Parental alienation occurs in families undergoing divorce when the custodial parent, possibly with the help of other family members, manipulates children into emotionally rejecting the noncustodial parent and showing a variety of negative emotions toward them that may include fear, hostility, anger, disrespect, or disobedience. This often leads to estrangement between a parent and their children.

When in the throes of a divorce, parents have been known to hurl all kinds of terrible accusations at each other, including child abuse and more. Naturally, the children involved hear this; children know much more about their parents than we think they do. When one parent bad-mouths the other parent twenty-four hours a day, seven days a week, eventually the children begin to believe what they hear.

This is a common occurrence that can result in psychological harm to the child, and it is extremely difficult to counteract. It is uncommon for a judge to recognize parental alienation as an argument for changing custody of children from one parent to the other, for example, and the longer it goes on, the deeper and more profound the damage to the relationship between parent and child.

From the moment we split up, and probably even before that, Chelsea did everything she could to turn our son and daughter against me. I am certain that all the terrible allegations she made against me got back to them, even if she didn't sit Natasha and Vincenzo down and tell them directly. I am equally certain that she spoke ill of me to them on a regular basis while they were living with her and I couldn't respond or defend myself. That's just the kind of woman she was—and still is.

I always tried to do everything I could for my children. Vincenzo actually lived with me for almost a year when I was living in Nevada in 2010 and practicing in Arizona. He and I have always had a good relationship, despite his not coming to see me in the hospital in Florida.

Even when Chelsea was poisoning Natasha against me, I was never willing to fight back in kind. I think—and child psychologists agree—that parental alienation as practiced by my ex-wife is a form of abuse and has long-term deleterious effects on the mind and emotions of the child. Not only did Natasha grow up without a father, but she grew up with a false image of who her father was, thanks to her mother's constant campaign of rage, negativity, and psychological torment. I'm grateful that Natasha was able to extricate herself from that situation, and I'm glad we're repairing our relationship now.

Natasha was about fourteen when Chelsea and I divorced, and problems set in almost immediately. I have no idea what Chelsea said to her, but I know that she must have been pouring poison into my daughter's ears from the day I left. I also know that the problems between Chelsea and me, including her plans to murder me, made it impossible for me to maintain contact with either of my children, much less to present my own side of things to them. As a consequence, my daughter didn't speak to me at all until a few years ago, after a decade of separation. Indeed, she wound up taking Chelsea's side in such a way that I was denied custody or any kind of visitation rights.

Throughout all the chaos that Chelsea and others brought into my life—and even worse, throughout all my health problems and near-death experiences—I never heard a word from Natasha. It was like I didn't exist for her. Recently out of desperation, however, she reached out to me as part of her spiritual reawakening, and we have resumed our relationship.

I bear her no ill will, and indeed I am sympathetic to her. But the horrible things she said are still embedded in my memory and very difficult to forget. I know how much she had to put up with, living with her mother for so many years after our divorce.

When we reconciled in 2016, Natasha was twenty and had moved out of Chelsea's house. Her mother had received a diagnosis of bipolar disorder and schizoaffective disorder, and Natasha could no longer live with her. Chelsea had also returned to illicit drug use. She was smoking pot—she had probably never stopped—and was also using cocaine and methamphetamine, all in front of Natasha. Fortunately, my daughter refused to be dragged down into her mother's spiral of addiction, nor did she want anything to do with the low-life addicts with whom Chelsea was hanging around. So she moved out, placing herself in financial hardship in the process. She made no attempt to contact me at this point, so I was unable to offer her any assistance.

My relationship with my son, Vincenzo, wasn't harmed by the divorce. He was eighteen, six years older than Natasha, and more perceptive about things. Vincenzo was well aware that his mother was a pathological liar, and her other behavior was just as obvious to him. He also saw the way she responded to me, or to any criticism from anyone, flying into rages at the slightest provocation, so he always tried to stay as neutral as possible and avoid sending her over the edge. Still, there was a conflict between Vincenzo and Chelsea.

Both my son and my ex-wife had ADD/ADHD, and Chelsea would ridicule Vincenzo until he fell into depression. One day I heard her say to him, "You worthless piece of shit, you never help around the house, your grades are terrible, and you do nothing with your free time except cause havoc in this household with your sister. What good are you?" She was psychologically abusing him so badly that he became chronically depressed, and I was worried about potential suicidal ideation.

It got so severe that I sent Vincenzo to Culver Military Academy in Indiana just to separate the two of them. That was hard for me, because I had to travel hundreds of miles on weekends to see him march in parades. It was worth it, though, because I saw a young man with pride in himself, choosing to go into the academy's naval/nautical division! Vincenzo began to blossom and mature, because Chelsea was not there to ridicule him and make him feel like a piece of shit.

My parents would come up whenever they could to visit him and watch him on parade. I loved seeing them watch their grandson with smiles on their faces. I was proud of Vincenzo, and it was a good choice for him to be separated from that pathological beast Chelsea. He regained his confidence and developed a sense of self-worth again.

Vincenzo was eighteen at the time of the divorce, already close to adulthood, and he had grown up with me as a strong, present male role model. Adolescence, as we all know, is a fragile time in a child's life, a time when the influence of both parents is crucial. Vincenzo had the benefit of a two-parent household throughout his teenage years, but Natasha did not, which goes a long way toward explaining the difference in my relationships with my son and my daughter.

CHAPTER TWENTY

Bernie the Blade

Recovering from surgery can be a terrible challenge. As the body heals, people often feel great pain, which is one of the reasons the opiate problem is so severe these days. Patients are prescribed drugs that are too strong and addictive, so they develop dependencies that can last for years and totally destroy their lives. Personally, I don't do well with drugs of any kind, so I avoided painkillers after my spinal surgery. The pain in the first few weeks after the operation was nearly unbearable, but I suffered through it because I knew the risk of addiction.

Typically, the worst pain from spinal fusion surgery lasts only about four weeks and continues to decrease gradually after that, though some people experience pain for as long as six months. Doctors typically recommend that patients avoid lifting heavy weights, bending too much, or twisting their backs during the recovery period, so that they'll heal properly.

This is especially true when they're prescribed a brace or body cast, as I was.

Unfortunately, I needed to move everything from my former office out of storage and into my new office, which had to be done slowly and carefully to avoid injuring my spine again. I was also undergoing outpatient physical therapy at Canyon Meadows Medical Center, to help me learn to walk again and regain strength in my legs. Although I had been taken immediately into surgery upon suffering my spinal injury, the damage to the nerves was severe. When you're coming back from spinal cord surgery, especially when you have osteoporosis, you have to rethink actions that you'd always taken for granted—sitting, standing, walking, lying down, and lifting, pushing, or pulling. You have to move more carefully and think about what you're doing before you do it. In some ways it's like tai chi or yoga, in that it forces you to be conscious of your movements and the way your body takes up space in the physical universe.

Many of us don't think about our bodies until they're injured. We go through our lives doing things without extra effort, and our limbs simply respond to our commands. But because of the accidents I've suffered, the long time I spent recovering from my spinal injury, and my injuries described at the beginning of this book, I'm extremely conscious of my body's frailty and vulnerability. I believe that this, in turn, makes me a better doctor.

Many doctors, and surgeons in particular, seem to have a kind of disrespect for the body. If a part isn't working properly, you simply cut it out or off. Surgeons can be extremely callous with their patients, showing little concern for their well-being or how long it may take the patient to recover from the treatment to which they've been subjected. In contrast, I always take the patient's recovery into account when deciding on a surgical strategy.

I work hard to be minimally invasive, leave the smallest possible scar, and do as little damage to the patient's body as possible, and I work in a way that allows for the easiest and least painful recovery. I have operated on tens of thousands of people who have been able to literally walk from the operating room to the recovery suite after the procedure, rather than knocking them unconscious, slicing them to bits, and sending them off with the attitude that they're someone else's problem now.

I was living in Clark County, Nevada, while recovering from surgery and waiting to start work at Canyon Meadows, and every day I drove past the Colorado River. Although I could tell that my condition was improving, therapy was difficult and the pain was extraordinary. There were days where I really felt like I couldn't take it anymore, and this was one of those days.

I had just returned from a physical therapy session at Canyon Meadows, and I was questioning whether it was all worth it. I was all but incapacitated, wrapped in a cast, and unable to see patients or earn a living. I had been in a terrible, nearly life-threatening car accident, which had only served to make my vindictive ex-wife and her lawyers even more angry and intent on persecuting me. It was a lot to deal with, and I was coming unglued, suffering from depression and stress, and searching for a way out.

Pulling the car off the road, I parked beside the Colorado River and just sat there all alone, thinking. *How long is this going to take? When am I going to be able to get back to work? I've spent my whole life trying to help people, and what has it gotten me?*

Finally I decided I had to do something drastic, so I got out of the car, removed my cast, and tossed it on the seat. Then I removed most of my clothes, kicked off my shoes, walked down to the river, and jumped in wearing just my underwear.

The Colorado River is not a slow-moving trickle of water. It's a powerful, rushing river with a current that can be fierce at times. I was taking my life in my hands. I could have been swept along and dragged under the water, or even slammed against a rock, which might have further injured my spine or knocked me unconscious. But I couldn't just keep going like I had been. I had to take charge and stop being a spectator in my own life. I believe in God, and I believe that nothing can change his plans for us.

I began to swim. I've always enjoyed swimming and I'm a strong swimmer, but this was about more than pleasure. This was about bringing myself back to life. It was autumn, and the water was cold and brisk, which kept me energized and focused on moving. The water enveloped me and wanted to move me downstream, far away from my car, so I stroked against the current with all my strength. My arms were stronger than my legs, but soon the core muscles in my back and abdomen began to respond and keep my lower limbs from flopping loosely in the water. It was like being in an infinity pool. It was better for me than anything I'd been doing with the hospital therapy team, as helpful and kind as they were. Besides, I had my osteoporosis to deal with, and the beautiful sunshine in Arizona could potentially help me heal faster.

I swam for hours, and the next day I returned and did it again. I began to swim every day for as long as I could. I was coming out of the water shaking with the exertion, but each time I did it, I could feel myself growing stronger, more alert, more in tune with my surroundings. My attitude grew stronger and more positive every day, and more importantly I could feel my confidence returning. I was enjoying the sunrises and sunsets, the quiet surroundings where I could meditate and feel myself in tune with nature. I was happier, more excited to get out of bed in the morning, and more convinced that soon, I would be back at Canyon Meadows Medical Center—not as a patient, but as a valued member of the surgical team, seeing patients and helping them recover from their own illnesses. I would be doing what I was born to do, what my family had been doing since the 1500s.

As I was swimming with all my might in the Colorado River, I started to have memories of various episodes that had brought me to my present situation. Sometimes searching our past experiences gives us the strength to overcome present challenges. Our subconscious mind gives strength to our conscious mind to overcome the obstacles facing us. Swimming vigorously, I remembered an episode that occurred while I was an intern and made me a stronger surgeon. So I was connecting the strength of my recuperation, which was a hurdle in itself, to the hurdles that I had experienced in my life and occupation.

As an intern at Brookdale Hospital Medical Center doing my first year of training in 1983, I was blessed with the opportunity to be in a setting where I had a lot of experience with trauma. One senior resident in particular stood out to me. They called him "Bernie the blade," because he always kept a sterile scalpel in a test tube in his coat pocket, just in case an emergency trauma occurred. Bernie was one of the best surgeons I've ever known.

It was my first week as an intern at Brookdale, in New York City, having returned to the United States after earning my medical degree in Italy. I was totally naïve as an intern, especially since nothing that they teach you in medical school and during your clinical clerkships prepares you for doing your residency. I was rotating through various services, in general surgery at the time, and on call in the emergency room. It was somewhere around two o'clock in the morning, and I was suturing minor lacerations with patients lined up down the corridor.

I was taking care of a cabdriver who had been rear-ended by another car and thrown against the dashboard. The sun visor had been partially down and actually scalped the cabdriver; his skull was totally exposed and his hair was flipped over like a toupee. He wasn't in any pain, and he joked with me by flipping his scalp back and forth, saying "Look what happened to me, Doc!" He was quite funny, and we talked as I worked on him.

I was diligently cleaning and suturing this man's scalp in a bloodless environment, which was taking quite some time. The door was open, and I could see the entire emergency room, including the triage desk. I noticed a black gentleman, a Rastafarian, enter the emergency room, which was quite packed at that time. Under his jacket, a black leather trench coat, I could see what looked like a gun. The beads in his dreadlocks were making noise as he yelled at the nurse to get her attention. She gave him some forms to fill out and then, without looking at him, told him to have a seat.

The man began shouting out loud, "I need to see a doctor now!" But the nurse, who seemed rather overwhelmed, kept telling him to take a seat, fill out the paperwork, and she would be right with him. I was watching him attentively as I worked on the cabdriver.

Then the man said to the nurse, "You don't understand. I need to see a doctor *now*." He reached toward his left pocket and proceeded to take out what looked like a gun. The patient that I was suturing said to me, "Looks like you got trouble, Doc."

The nurse still wasn't paying any attention to the man, until he yanked a shiny metal object—which turned out to be an ice pick, not a gun—right out of his chest. Blood spurted all over the nurse like a fountain, drenching her and her paperwork. Covered with bright red blood, she yelled, "Code blue."

I quickly ran to help, just as the gentleman turned and spurted blood all over the emergency room floor and walls. As I got close to him, covered with blood, he collapsed into my arms. The other emergency room personnel helped me get him on a stretcher and the nurses started to check his vital signs. I quickly tore off the man's shirt and realized that this was a penetrating trauma secondary to an ice pick wound within the left chest wall. I told the nurses to type and cross match the patient for ten units of blood. Security had notified all surgical personnel on the house staff to report to the emergency room stat.

The trauma room was crowded with personnel as lines were started on the patient. In his rebellious state, he was telling everyone to go fuck themselves. When someone is losing that much blood, circulation to the brain decreases and the patient easily becomes confused.

While I was trying to cut the pants off the gentleman to do a cut down on his leg veins, Bernie the blade nonchalantly waltzed into the trauma room. Seeing all the commotion, he patted me on the back and asked, "What've you got here?"

I quickly replied, "Penetrating trauma to the chest with a possible collapsed lung and cardiac tamponade."

When Bernie asked about the man's vital signs, I replied 100/60 with a pulse of 120. He quickly told me that my assessment was wrong, because if the man did have a tamponade, he would've flatlined by then. That was my educated guess, but I was just a measly intern.

Bernie instructed me to continue doing what I was doing, and he asked the nurses for a CVP line. Anesthesia was called, and everyone was working as a team. The patient was becoming more abusive with the staff, thrashing his hands and legs around as if he was trying to hit someone. Bernie remained calm and started to place the CVP line on the right side of the patient's neck as I proceeded to do a cut down on the man's greater saphenous vein with IV tubing. Suddenly the patient bit Bernie's hand, drawing blood and taking out a chunk of skin, which he then spit at the nearest nurse.

Bernie was in excruciating pain and totally pissed off. He threw the lines on the floor and jumped on top of the patient's chest with his knee on the man's abdomen. Putting one hand around the patient's throat, Bernie yelled, "If you do that one more time, motherfucker, you will be kissing God soon!"

No sooner did he say those words than the patient flatlined. Bernie nonchalantly got off the patient's chest, walked to his white jacket, which was hanging on another gurney, took out his test tube, and cracked it open against the patient's stretcher to remove the blade. Then he instructed everyone except me to stand back, and he told me to quickly put on some gloves.

With one quick stroke, Bernie made an incision through the patient's skin, muscle, and ribs, right down to his lungs, and exposed his heart, which was pulsating blood like a fountain. Then he turned to me and said, "You were right. It's a tamponade." As he evacuated the clotted blood from the area, a small hole became apparent within the patient's heart.

As blood continued to spurt onto Bernie and the nurses, he instructed me to place my left index finger into this hole. I quickly did so, and the bleeding stopped. By that time, we had approximately four units of blood and two units of fresh frozen plasma running into different lines. The patient's blood pressure improved, though it was still low, and Bernie instructed someone to call the operating room and have them ready.

With my finger in the man's chest, I could feel his pulsating heart. It was a strange sensation, having somebody's heart contracting around my left index finger. When I asked Bernie what I should do next, he quickly replied, "Just keep your finger there". I was drenched in blood and sweat, and my adrenaline was at its peak.

The patient's blood pressure was improving, so the stretcher bars came up and the two of us were taken up the elevator to the operating room. Bernie took the next elevator and met us there as I kept my finger in the man's heart. I was surrounded by people, also covered with blood, holding up bags of blood and fluids, and we all looked at each other and started to laugh at the situation. One nurse said, "It must be a full moon tonight."

Then the elevator doors opened again, and the anesthesia team arrived. They quickly helped to wheel the patient and me, sitting on top of him with my finger in his heart, into the nearest operating room. Meanwhile an overwhelming sense of strength came upon me, like I had never before experienced.

Bernie was already scrubbing, and the other residents were quickly preparing the Betadine around me. The rest of the team was prepping the patient's neck, chest, and abdomen, and the anesthesia team head intubated him.

As Bernie entered the room, he asked me, "How many cardiac tamponades have you done?"

"None," I replied, "but I've seen two."

"That's good enough for me," he said. "You have exactly thirty seconds to scrub and gown yourself." Then he instructed me to remove my finger, and as I did so, he placed his own sterile finger into the patient's heart, started antibiotics, and waited for me to return.

My adrenaline level was at an all-time high, with my heart racing at approximately 120 beats a minute. This was my first week as an intern, and I was intensely focused on the situation at hand. I quickly scrubbed, and as I reentered the operating room, the nurses splashed alcohol on my hands, placed the gown over my arms, and slapped the gloves on my hands.

Bernie said, "That was forty seconds. You're late!" Then he removed his finger from the heart and told me to "Fix this man. Now!" With that, he folded his hands on his belly and watched to see what my next step would be.

I quickly placed my finger back in the patient's heart to stop the bleeding and requested surgical pledgets, sutures, and retraction. With one finger in the heart, I used my other hand to suture the hole shut by reapproximating the two opposing edges of the circular wound. When the sutures were in place, I gingerly tied them down over the pledgets to complete the operation. Then I waited and watched the area that I had sutured, looking for any bleeding, but there was none. We had transfused six liters of blood and four units of fresh frozen plasma, and the patient's vital signs were stable.

When I looked up at Bernie, he exclaimed, "Good job! Now close him up."

As Bernie left me alone to complete the operation, he called back from the operating room door, "You were right. Do you realize what you've done"?

I shrugged and asked, "No. What?"

He replied, "You just saved this bastard's life." Then he glanced down at his injured hand and walked out the door.

A sense of total fulfillment came over me—a feeling of success under emergency conditions with a critical patient. Throughout the situation, I had experienced enormous strength and a sense of empowerment. Any doctor has that experience many times during his or her career, and that was one of the many glorious moments that have been preserved in my memory banks.

As I swam as hard as I could, I remembered the adrenaline rush and strength that had overcome me during that unique experience. All the while, I told myself that I was going to get better and stronger as time went on!

Once I began swimming, as well as continuing my prescribed physical therapy regimen, my recovery seemed to fly by. My spinal injury had occurred in September, and by January I was ready to go back to work. It was exciting to be in a new state, at a new hospital, and preparing to work with an entirely new team. I could see a bright future for myself in Arizona.

Little did I know how bad things would get when I met Dr. Morelli. That man, his wife, Margaret, and his associates would prove to be some of the worst enemies I have encountered in all my years on Earth. Soon their attempts to destroy me would rival even Chelsea's—and that was before they joined forces with her in a truly horrifying and mind-boggling conspiracy to ruin my medical career, destroy my personal life, bankrupt me financially, and even send me to prison. All this would come to pass sooner than I could possibly have imagined as I swam the Colorado River that fall, recovering my strength and preparing for the next phase of my life and career.

CHAPTER TWENTY-ONE

A Real Psychopath

In January 2010, I finally completed my physical therapy program. Thanks to the staff at Canyon Meadows Medical Center and my own regimen of swimming in the Colorado River, my spine was healed and I had fully regained my ability to walk and perform my duties as a surgeon. I was still under treatment for the osteoporosis that I had developed from long hours in the operating room, but that wouldn't keep me from getting back to work. I had patients to see.

I joined the staff that month, getting a fresh start at the beginning of a new year—or so I thought. My office was next door to the main building, and at first everyone was welcoming, friendly, and helpful. The nurses and administrators extended me every courtesy and did all they could to get me settled into the routine of the facility.

Like any large organization, hospitals are complex systems with dozens of overlapping departments, each with its own agenda and procedures, yet all contributing to the safe and efficient operation of the whole. If one department breaks down or ceases to operate at its best, the entire system can begin to splinter, resulting in danger to the patients. For example, during a laparoscopic procedure on a gallbladder, a complication arose and the surgeon had to convert to an open approach, but the room hadn't been set up for that. The surgeon intern became abusive to the nursing staff, which created fear and confusion, thus slowing down the operative intervention. This will become important in the story I'm about to tell you.

Despite the generally positive attitude with which I was greeted by the staff, there was something in the air at Canyon Meadows that I just couldn't put my finger on. It was like a fog of toxicity that hung over the entire hospital, giving every interaction an edge of hostility and fear. People seemed to be constantly looking over their shoulder, making sure they weren't doing something that would anger someone else or even jeopardize their own job.

One of the first people I met was a fellow urologist. He was initially pleasant and friendly; we discussed our backgrounds, as doctors do, and he even mentioned having been through the same training program as me. I could not have anticipated, getting to know him then, that I would eventually be forced to report him to the federal government for Medicare fraud.

Even Dr. Morelli, whom I met within the first day or two, seemed fine. A short, sickly, thin, pale, balding man, he emitted a tremendous wave of negative energy. The staff seemed to flinch away from him, or they'd try to look busy as he passed, as though they feared being drawn into a conversation with him. But I didn't pay attention to these warning signs; to me, he seemed fine.

Morelli was a proctologist and general surgeon, and we shared the mentality and attitude common to people who cut other people open for a living. He also was of Italian descent, if not 100 percent Italian like me, so it seemed reasonable that we should get along. That only made it more shocking when he turned out to be such an implacable and merciless enemy.

I soon discovered that Dr. Morelli was an egomaniac and narcissist with a truly poisonous personality. It was Morelli haunting the halls of Canyon Meadows Medical Center, creating the toxic atmosphere that everyone else had to breathe in and work through.

When I first met Morelli, he seemed fairly benign. My initial impression was that he was a decent guy, cunning but cordial, until you got to know him better. Upon learning that my last name was Italian, like his, he said, "Nice to meet you, fellow Italian *paisano*." He was by no means knowledgeable about Italian language or customs, but we had a cordial introduction.

Despite being an average surgeon at best—and, I would eventually discover, something much more dangerous—Morelli had worked hard to create the illusion that he was a medical genius whom Canyon Meadows was lucky to have. He saw the hospital as his personal kingdom, and through sheer force of will and intimidation of everyone around him, he erected a barrier of fear that prevented the administration, nursing staff, or anyone else from resisting him.

Dr. Morelli was a marginal doctor who had begun his career in Needles, California, right across the desert from Mojave Valley, Arizona. The hospital where he started had only three beds and, I believe, one operating room. I assume that's the only place in the country where he could possibly have gotten privileges. After Canyon Meadows Medical Center was built, he got his Arizona license and moved his practice to Fort Mojave. Morelli definitely wouldn't have been successful starting out in a big city, where he would've been swallowed alive because of his incompetence.

It was a well-known fact that both Dr. Morelli and his wife, Margaret, were morally unscrupulous and believed themselves to be above everybody else. If you crossed them, they would hunt you down. One of my friends who was on the board of trustees crossed the Morellis one day in an argument. That weekend Dr. Morelli went hunting and shot an elk, and the next day an elk's head was found on my friend's front doorstep. Just like in *The Godfather*, the message was clear: Don't mess with me.

The Black Rose, a club in Bullhead City, was known to host orgies and illicit sexual escapades. I was told by numerous people that both Dr. Morelli and Margaret would frequent this club, along with a few other doctors in Mojave Valley, before I arrived in town. This just goes to show you their lack of morals.

There's no question in my mind that Margaret would use her body to persuade people, probably including Connor Truman, to perform illegal acts. Truman has done horrendous things, using his legal license for his own illicit gain and conspiring with the Morellis, which he has openly admitted in court, while also conspiring with my ex-wife and Veronica Fischer, her lawyer.

Dr. Morelli was one of the angriest men I have ever met. He had a breathtakingly short temper and would respond to the slightest stress or provocation with outbursts of violence. There were many stories of him throwing surgical instruments at nurses, in the middle of operations, if he thought they weren't doing things the right way—his way.

Anyone below him on the organizational chain feared for their job every time they had to have a conversation with the man, never mind share an operating room with him. What choice did they have, though? He had wormed his way into real power within the hospital, and it was going to take something truly extraordinary to get him out—if anyone was even willing to try.

As I said, Morelli was initially friendly with me. He must have been sizing me up, deciding whether I was someone he could co-opt and lure to his side, or if I was an enemy to be destroyed. Once my practice got underway and I was actively seeing patients, he made his decision.

I was lulled into a false sense of security, because it took me a few months to get settled in and really start seeing patients in earnest. I didn't experience the full effect of Dr. Morelli's madness until I started doing major surgery at Canyon Meadows.

My father, with whom I had shared a practice in New York, was a pioneer of ambulatory surgery, and he taught me everything he knew. We were a team of experts, recognized internationally for our ability to perform hernia procedures on patients under local anesthesia and have them walk away to recover. People would fly to New York specifically to see us for hernia operations, or to have us repair hernia operations botched by other doctors, all while they were awake and lucid.

When some of those patients found out that I was at Canyon Meadows, they began to call me and come from New York, or Europe, or wherever they lived. Others were new to me, but they had heard about my techniques and sterling reputation. Hernia surgeries are not a full-time job for a urological surgeon, but I've done thousands of them in my lifetime. In fact, I've written numerous medical papers on hernia repair techniques and even a chapter in a medical textbook on hernias. I could perform a hernia operation with one eye shut.

When Dr. Morelli saw that I was beginning to perform these surgeries at Canyon Meadows, he reacted like a furious child, as if I was stepping into his corner of a nursery school sandbox and playing with his toys. My very first hernia procedure there involved a patient who had flown in from Europe seeking my help. He was literally in the holding area when I discovered that my operating room time had been removed from the schedule!

I immediately took the issue to administration, but Morelli didn't care that a patient was awaiting surgery. He said, "There's no fuckin' way you're gonna do a hernia." I suspect that he was even angrier because I had listed the procedure as requiring only local anesthesia, when he preferred to completely knock people out.

Chris Johns, the administrator, and Morelli hated each other. In fact, it was well known that they had actually gotten into a physical altercation. Morelli had punched Johns out in the parking lot, an attack that was witnessed by Harris Letterman, an outstanding surgeon from Harvard—and another of Morelli's victims. Johns had been showing a new surgical candidate around the hospital, and Morelli's fear of competition had driven him into a rage. It was evident that he kept his despicable activities secret, because of his Machiavellian approach to eliminating all potential competitors who might have discovered his corruption.

The incident with my hernia patient had only served to make the enmity between the two men even more bitter. Johns could barely stand the sight of Morelli, so when presented with the opportunity to knock him down a peg, he found it irresistible. I was given permission to perform that hernia operation, as well as any others that patients might request. That's when my feud with Morelli began in earnest.

Things got worse as I began to perform more difficult procedures. I was doing things in the operating room that had never been done in that entire region, including Phoenix. One of my specialties was the creation of what is known as an orthotopic neobladder.

Bladder cancer is extremely common—the ninth-most common cancer worldwide, and the second-most common urological malignancy, after prostate cancer. When bladder cancer reaches a certain point, treatment requires cystectomy, the removal of the bladder, which obviously causes major life changes for the patient, including the need to create a stoma and an ileal conduit. A section of the intestine is cut away and connected to the ureters, tubes that carry urine out of the kidneys, and then attached to the stoma, a hole in the abdomen. A bag to collect the urine is then attached to that opening. This can be psychologically damaging and even cause depression, because people simply don't like the idea of urinating into a bag that then has to be manually emptied for the rest of their life.

The orthotopic neobladder presents an alternative solution. After the patient's bladder is removed, a new bladder is constructed using a section of intestine, thus allowing the patient to urinate or use a catheter just like anyone else. There's no need for a bag or external drainage, and nobody needs to know that your bladder has been removed.

I had spent a significant amount of time perfecting my technique for building orthotopic neobladders. I would use about thirty centimeters of the patient's small and large bowel for the construction, depending on how large the capacity of the bladder needed to be. I would build what is known as a Mainz pouch, using small and large intestine as well as a portion of the colon. The colon contains smooth muscle fibers called taenia, into which I would implant the ureters to prevent refluxing. That way, urine would flow only downward, rather than backing up into the kidneys when the bladder was full.

When my patients were fully healed, their bladder capacity was more than a liter in some cases. They were able to urinate using a valsalva maneuver, a kind of squeezing abdominal pressure. Or they could do intermittent catheterization, inserting the catheter only when the bladder's full, rather than leaving it in all the time, which carries the risk of urinary tract infections. As a result, my patients led more normal and healthy lives than people who had to rely on an external bag. They were able to retain their dignity and avoid the depression and mental stress I described above.

The first time I performed an orthotopic neobladder procedure at Canyon Meadows, the news traveled all over, to Bullhead City and Fort Mohave and the surrounding areas.

So many nurses and doctors wanted to see the procedure that the observation gallery was completely full, and there was a line from the operating room all the way down the hall. There was even a story in the local newspaper about the new doctor in town, and how I had brought a new medical technique to their community. The spotlight was on me, not Dr. Morelli, and his fragile ego couldn't cope. From that moment, he became a seething, bitter man who was determined to bring me down.

CHAPTER TWENTY-TWO

Shark Bait

Dr. Morelli's naked hostility toward me was obvious from the moment I began to perform complex surgeries at Canyon Meadows Medical Center. One day when I was doing a laparoscopic prostatectomy, he approached me and said, "You don't have privileges to do a laparoscopic prostatectomy."

I responded, "Dr. Morelli, you gave me privileges to do laparoscopy, which entitles me to do various interventions, including laparoscopic prostatectomy."

"I did?" he asked.

"Yes, you did," I confirmed, "and my privileges were approved by the medical executive committee."

What I was doing was beyond his capabilities, which caused him to lose status within the hospital. He was still the chief of surgery, which meant that I worked under him, but he was a maniac prone to screaming fits and violent outbursts. In contrast, I was friendly with the nurses and administrators, and I tried to keep things running as smoothly as possible. Who do you think the staff liked better?

It was an incredibly awkward situation. I was showing up to work every day and trying to help my patients, knowing all the while that my adversary resented my skills and professional accomplishments. Morelli bore me a personal grudge because I was good at my job! We argued regularly over issues large and small, though we always seemed to resolve things in the moment. But when I added it all up, it was the dictionary definition of a hostile work environment.

I put up with it as best I could, keeping my head down and focusing on giving my patients the best care possible. But when Morelli and I were forced into proximity, like when we had operations scheduled for the same block of time, things were always on a razor's edge. On the other hand, if we hadn't been scheduled to work at the same time, I might never have discovered what a bad doctor he really was.

Immediately after surgeons perform procedures, they're required to dictate reports that must be transcribed and entered into their patients' medical records as soon as possible. One day I was in the dictation room, dictating notes on a long and complex operation that I had just completed. Dr. Morelli came in to dictate a procedure of his own, but he finished quickly and rushed out of the room as though he had somewhere important to be.

His behavior made me suspicious, and I glanced at the board on the wall where each surgeon's cases for the day were listed. I was astonished to see that he had something like fifteen colonoscopies scheduled, plus some other procedures as well. A properly executed colonoscopy requires anywhere from half an hour to a full hour. I had no idea what was going on, but I didn't have much time to think about it. Five minutes later, he came back into the room and began dictating a new procedure. He quickly spat out his notes on whatever he'd just done, threw a venomous glance in my direction, and was gone again.

I thought, *What the hell? How can he be doing this many colonoscopies? Does he have them all lined up in a row or something?* It wasn't even noon. If the records were to be believed, Morelli was cranking out those procedures at incomprehensible speed. It was impossible for him to be providing high-quality care to anyone that fast.

I didn't want to get into it with him, though. Our working relationship was bad enough already, so I decided to just keep my head down and do my own work. But once you become aware of something in your environment, it starts to gradually reveal itself in more and more detail, until it's all you can see. Then you can't believe that you never noticed it before.

I began to hear rumors that a lot of the patients on whom Dr. Morelli had performed his high-speed colonoscopies were showing up at the other local hospital, Bullhead City Medical Center. Over at BCMC, the story went, these people were being admitted for bleeding or other complications. When the surgeon there, Dr. Wes Brown, saw them on an emergency basis, he would either do a colonoscopy or, in many cases, open them up because they had bleeding and cancer of the colon.

It became all too clear that Dr. Morelli was simply not performing the procedures for which he was taking credit and billing. He was committing fraud—and even worse, he was endangering people's lives.

I began to surreptitiously approach the operating room technicians with whom Dr. Morelli was working on these so-called colonoscopies. When one of those techs came to my office as a patient, I asked him, "When you do colonoscopies with Dr. Morelli, do you always see the cecum?"

After thinking hard, he said, "You know, come to think of it, I've never seen the cecum in all of the cases that I've done with Morelli."

I did everything I could to keep Morelli from finding out about my unofficial investigation, but eventually I knew he was aware of my activities, so I began to watch my back in earnest. It is always a doctor's responsibility to be aware of patient endangerment issues and report them to the proper authorities when necessary.

There's one easy way to know whether a colonoscopy has been performed properly. The portal where the small intestine joins the large intestine is called the cecum. If you don't see the cecum on the screen, you haven't performed a complete colonoscopy. So when I spoke to the OR techs who worked with Dr. Morelli on his procedures, I asked them one question: "Did you see the cecum?"

Not one of them said yes. One tech even wound up testifying to the Arizona attorney general about his fraudulent activities. She told me that she never saw the cecum the entire time she did colonoscopies with Morelli, and every other tech with whom I spoke told me the same story.

As if that wasn't bad enough, he wasn't preserving records of what he was doing. A colonoscopy requires the insertion of a camera into the patient's alimentary canal, and the doctor observes the camera's journey on a monitor. But Dr. Morelli was not recording the footage, so there was no record of what he was doing—or not doing.

Another aspect of the colonoscopy procedure is the taking of tissue samples and sending them for analysis. Morelli would take normal mucosa from a patient, but label it a polyp when it was sent to the pathology department for biopsy.

A pathologist at Canyon Meadows actually approached him and asked him point-blank, "Why is it, Dr. Morelli, that you do so many colonoscopies, but you have the lowest yield when it comes to picking up cancers or any kind of pathology? All your patients seem to be perfectly healthy, way out of line with statistical averages. And any pathology that you do report turns out to be normal mucosa when subjected to analysis. Do you have any explanation for this?"

Within seventy-two hours, Dr. Morelli had gone to administration and demanded that the pathologist be fired, but he didn't stop there. The man actually had to move away, because Morelli wasn't going to stop until he destroyed the man's reputation and career. I should have realized that he would do the same thing to me given the chance, but I was more concerned about patient welfare than the state of my own career. I had to keep investigating.

It was clear to me that Dr. Morelli was not performing colonoscopies the way every other surgeon does, and that his patients were subsequently going to BCMC. In some cases, they were even dying from colon cancer that he had failed to detect, either through incompetence or deliberate negligence. I didn't yet know which, but it didn't matter.

I drove over to BCMC and had a closed-door meeting with Dr. Wes Brown, a fellow general surgeon. He told me, "This guy is a malignancy himself! I don't know what he's doing to these people, but it's not a colonoscopy, because I'm taking care of all the trash that he's leaving out there."

I thought, *This is not right. I have to do something.*

I must briefly digress. Just before I reported the truth to the federal government, I felt it was my responsibility to take the information that I had accumulated to the chief of staff at BCMC. His name was Robert Yarbrough, and he was the chief of anesthesia as well as a good friend—or so I thought.

Over breakfast one Saturday, I told Yarbrough what my investigation had revealed. I had spoken to numerous OR technicians and other general surgeons, and in my position as chairman of surgery at Canyon Meadows Medical Center, I had access to Dr. Morelli's old charts. All of this supported the conclusion that it was impossible for him to perform these colonoscopies in the short period of time he was claiming. And that didn't even take into account the deaths of which Wes had personal knowledge from cleaning up Morelli's disasters.

When I spoke to Dr. Yarbrough, I didn't know that he and Morelli were best friends. When I told him about the necessity of conducting a full investigation at BCMC, he said, "Dino, just drop it."

In February 2013, I was notified by Ted Paxton, who was both a nurse and a lawyer, that Morelli had it out for me. Paxton provided me with the following document, which shows how corrupt Morelli was:

February 25, 2013

To whom it may concern:

Dr. Morelli spoke to me privately in the dictation room in the surgical department at the hospital medical center sometime after the

arrival of Dr. Panvini but before the summer of
2011. I had knocked and entered in the normal
course of my duties as an operating room
circulator, to tell him that his room was ready
for surgery. He motioned for me to come in and
said, "Shut the door."

He said, "I hate that bastard. Don't you?" I
asked, "To whom are you referring?" He said,
"Him. Panvini. He's out to get me, the son of
a bitch." I said, "Really? I don't know that."
He said, "Yes, that fucking son of a bitch. I'd
like to really get him, but I can't. He's after
me, but I don't know why." He went on to say
that "someone else" could call the "state" and
report Panvini. "I would do it myself," he said,
"but I can't, you understand. There's nothing
preventing you from calling though." It was
clear that Morelli wanted me to call a false report
to the state and federal authorities, implicating
Dr. Panvini in malpractice or fraud. I tried to
say that I wasn't qualified, from my point of
view, to judge whether Dr. Panvini's surgery
was up to standard, and I tried to make a joke.
He said, "I'm serious." He said he would tell me
everything I needed to know—the number to
call, who to ask for, and what to say. I asked,
"What do you mean by *what to say?*" He said,
"It wouldn't matter. That's the only way to stop
that son of a bitch." I said that I didn't want any

part of anything like that, that it sounded like a bad idea, and then I left. It was clear to me that Morelli very much wanted me to call in a false report to the authorities and medical licensing board, condemning Dr. Panvini for fraud and/or malpractice.

Several weeks later, Morelli repeated his entreaty to call the state on Dr. Panvini. I got the impression that Dr. Morelli had forgotten that he'd already asked me about it. Again, he tried to say that he "would call" himself, "but couldn't." Again it was clear that he wanted to make a false report implicating Dr. Panvini, with the express purpose of harassing him via medical licensing board and state/federal investigations. Again, he would supply me with all the necessary phone numbers and contact persons, plus the "facts" of the allegations to be reported. This time, he stated that he was "serious," that he "meant business," and that if I would do this for him, he would "make it worth my while." It was clear that Morelli was offering to pay me for calling in a false report on Dr. Panvini. Again, I said I didn't want any part of the idea, and I further stated that calling in a false report would be an ill-advised course of action, that he should abandon it, that it wasn't what any reputable attorney would advise, and that he should consult his attorney before making any reports. Then I left.

Signed,

Ted Paxton, RN, JD

This shows you the severity of both the pathology and the Machiavellian actions that this man intended against me. He would do anything to destroy my reputation, and it was rather obvious that Morelli had been contacted by Yarbrough.

I was befuddled, so I didn't discuss it with Yarbrough any further and we continued to have a cordial breakfast. About ten days later, we were operating together; he was the anesthesiologist on a case that I was doing. He offered to take me and MJ, a friend of his who was also an anesthesiologist, deep-sea fishing in Costa Rica. I said that would be great; I love deep-sea fishing.

Several days later I was sent a ticket to Costa Rica with a handwritten note from Yarbrough that read, "Let's catch some fish." I opened the envelope, examined the contents, and realized that it was a one-way ticket. By that time, I had discovered that he and Morelli were good friends. The thought raced through my mind that they were probably in collusion, and now Morelli knew everything and had probably told Yarbrough to take care of it.

The one-way ticket was ominous. Was I to become chum for sharks in the Atlantic Ocean, out there all alone? I called Yarbrough and told him that I had received the ticket in the mail, but that it seemed to be one-way; there was no return flight listed. He said that he had intentionally left the return trip open-ended.

That sounded fishy to me, no pun intended. So I graciously said, "Thank you, but I've got a lot of things going on that week and cases that have to be taken care of."

Interestingly enough, I had a case over at BCMC during the dates that had been earmarked for the trip to Costa Rica, and Yarbrough and MJ were there, too! They never went to Costa Rica. Obviously they had been planning the trip specifically for me. Was it to shut me up, or to end my investigation? Many thoughts went through my mind, but I'm glad I didn't go. Apparently I had been poking a beehive, and I didn't want to get stung. I chalked that experience up to my gut feeling and sixth sense.

I ended up making a report to the Arizona medical licensing board and attorney general, and then I filed a "qui tam" action against Morelli under the False Claims Act. That allows a whistleblower to file suit on behalf of the federal government and receive a percentage of any penalty levied against the defendant. In my case, I asserted that Dr. Morelli was committing Medicare fraud by billing the government for colonoscopies that he wasn't performing.

Up to then, I had relied on people whom I thought were my friends to support me. But there's an old saying in Italy: "Friends are like umbrellas. When it rains, you can never find them." Many of my so-called friends were afraid of their own shadows. I won't list their names here, because they know who they are—and so does God.

By then I was working at both Canyon Meadows and BCMC. I handled most of my cases at Canyon Meadows, but sometimes BCMC doctors would ask me to come over and take care of patients there, and I would occasionally transfer a patient from one hospital to the other where there were beds available. I was also serving as head of the operating room safety committee at BCMC, so I obviously couldn't let someone get away with endangering patients. Something had to be done.

CHAPTER TWENTY-THREE

Medical Corruption

The conflict with Dr. Morelli continued to get worse, and I was deeply disturbed by his blatant medical negligence. He never expressed the slightest remorse for leaving patients untreated and effectively abandoning them to die, nor did he display any guilt about committing Medicare fraud on an almost industrial scale. Instead, he strutted through Canyon Meadows like it was his own private kingdom, reacting with rage anytime anyone dared to question him. When the situation hit home in a personal way, though, I was forced to intervene directly.

One day, I was talking to Olivia Rivers, the head nurse at BCMC, in her office. A nice woman, Olivia was highly competent in the way of all great head nurses. She ran her team with a mix of iron-willed discipline and genuine consideration for others—and where patients were concerned, she was fantastic. I really liked her, and I thought of her as one of the hospital's greatest assets.

Olivia told me, "My fiancé has familial adenomatous polyposis."

People who suffer from this extremely dangerous genetic condition develop polyps in the mucosa of the large intestine. These polyps are benign at first, but if they aren't treated, they will become malignant and turn into colon cancer. The older the patient is, the higher the risk of cancer; by age forty-five, the chance that a person with one variety of familial adenomatous polyposis will develop colon cancer is 87 percent. By age fifty, their risk rises to 93 percent. Because of this, people with this disorder need extremely careful and detailed colonoscopies.

When Olivia brought her fiancé to BCMC, she had asked for the best possible doctor to examine him. Most people who knew about the shoddy nature of Morelli's work were nursing assistants and technicians, low on the hospital totem pole. On the other hand, he had a lot of friends in the local medical community, and everyone she spoke to referred her to him.

Olivia told me, "My fiancé just had a colonoscopy with Dr. Morelli, and he didn't find anything!" She said it with a smile, like she was delivering good news.

I must have gone pale, because her expression quickly changed. I walked over and locked her office door. By the time I sat back down at her desk, she could tell something serious was on my mind.

"Olivia," I said, "I can't emphasize strongly enough how important this is. I need you to speak to Dr. Wes Brown. Ask him about Dr. Morelli. I also think it would be a good idea for you to get a copy of his operative report, and make note of the time in and time out for the entire procedure."

Olivia looked surprised, but she agreed to do as I advised. She spoke to Brown and asked for copies of both the operative report and the anesthesia record, and then we looked them over together. With colonoscopies, the operative report lists a literal "time in" and "time out," indicating when the scope goes into the patient's body and when it comes back out. The report on Olivia's fiancé showed a two-minute span between time in and time out. You can't do a colonoscopy in two minutes—it's impossible! In fact, you can't perform any kind of medical examination in such a short period of time. This was negligence and fraud—malpractice, plain and simple.

When Olivia read the report, she turned as white as I had when I heard that Dr. Morelli had performed the procedure. "Oh my God," she said. "Oh my God, you were right. The colonoscopy only took two minutes." She knew that she needed to take action, but first she had to ensure that her fiancé got the treatment he needed from a doctor worthy of the name.

Olivia took him to another proctologist in another town. Just as they'd both expected, her fiancé did have polyps, but none were malignant and they were all removed.

With the immediate crisis behind her, Olivia began thinking about how Dr. Morelli could be stopped. She took it upon herself to start making copies of his procedures, saving the video to a personal external hard drive without his knowledge. She was careful about the chain of custody with this information, since it would have been a violation of patient confidentiality to share it with anyone else. She was simply gathering evidence for a future internal complaint.

Unfortunately the administration at BCMC, just like at Canyon Meadows, was on Morelli's side. BCMC's administrator, Max Lopez, was a particularly strong supporter and made sure that complaints were quashed and issues were swept under the rug. When Morelli and Lopez found out about Olivia's recordings, she was ordered to stop, and it was made clear that her position was at risk if she continued to cause problems for one of their star doctors. She became uneasy about working in a place with that kind of corrupt administration, and who could blame her?

My qui tam action against Dr. Morelli was made to go away, too. His father was a high-powered federal lawyer, and I have to assume he had a lot of friends in the federal government. The suit was swept under the rug and the file was sealed. I don't even know what's in the file; I'm legally constrained from seeing it, even though I brought the case in the first place.

To the best of my knowledge, Morelli was never found guilty, despite the countless witnesses looking forward to testifying against him with indisputable evidence. Perhaps there was some kind of under-the-table, back-room settlement, but I'm not aware of anything. It's all a corrupt mystery.

CHAPTER TWENTY-FOUR

Morelli's Exit

Of course, when I brought my legal action against Dr. Morelli, he went berserk. He was stressed out and abusive to everybody around him, including the hospital staff. One day when something wasn't going well in the operating room, he threw a scalpel against the wall, as though he was aiming directly at a target, and yelled, "Give me a fucking scalpel that works, you incompetent pieces of shit."

Morelli was able to make the qui tam lawsuit go away, probably with the help of his father, a retired federal lawyer. He was enraged that anyone would dare question his authority or try to stop him from conducting himself exactly as he saw fit. He was endangering patients on a daily basis, some of whom were desperately ill, but he strutted around the hospital like an emperor, yelling at the staff any time he didn't get his way.

Naturally the staff's fear of him only increased. No one was willing to challenge him; they only wanted to make sure they weren't in the room the next time he exploded.

Disgusted by it all, I was trying to focus on my own patients and do the best job I could for them. But the longer I stayed at Canyon Meadows, the more difficult it became to work. *What is it with this town?* I asked myself. *People are dying left and right, but no one seems willing to do a damn thing about it. What kind of power does he have over these people? Is it something in the drinking water?*

It soon became clear to me that it was all about money. Chris Johns, the administrator with whom Dr. Morelli had a terrible relationship—to the point that they had gotten into a physical altercation in the hospital parking lot—had finally had enough. He couldn't put up with the man's unethical, reckless, and dangerous behavior any longer, so he left.

The new CEO who took his place didn't know what was going on, and no one informed him. If they had, he might not have taken the job. But he was in charge, he was new, and he saw only the numbers on the financial spreadsheets. From his perspective, Dr. Morelli was a highly qualified, respected head of surgery performing a large number of colonoscopies and bringing in serious money for the hospital in the process. The new CEO wasn't going to rock the boat, which made it easy for Morelli to steamroll right over him and continue his criminal behavior.

Since the new administrator was allowing him to conduct himself with impunity, Dr. Morelli felt free to exact revenge on me for having notified the Arizona medical licensing board about him and filing the federal qui tam action against him. He saw me as his enemy, and he was determined to destroy me.

Morelli began to abuse his power as head of surgery. First he reduced the number of hours I could get an operating room for my patients by changing schedules and block times. He also told the head nurse and chief of staff to limit my operating room exposure. Because of the high profile and difficult cases I was working on, I was the hospital's highest earner, and he was trying to choke off that income stream out of personal animus.

When that wasn't enough to satisfy him, he began knocking my cases off the schedule completely. The chief of staff was Dr. Singh, a good friend of Dr. Morelli's. I had another patient come to see me for an orthotopic neobladder operation, but Dr. Morelli ordered Singh to cancel the procedure—and Singh obeyed. When I checked the schedule on the appointed day, it was gone. I believe he felt that by preventing me from performing the operation, he was not only punishing me for getting in his way, but also salvaging his own ego. After all, this was the procedure that had made me a star at Canyon Meadows. If I was kept out of the operating room, he would regain his status. That's how his diseased mind worked.

I wasn't going to let him force me out, though, because I had a patient to consider. I went immediately to the new administrator and asked, "What the hell is going on here? I'm being locked out of the operating room. I've performed this procedure here many times, and I've never faced this kind of behavior." Then I gave him an ultimatum: "Either you do something about this malignant surgeon, or I'm walking out the door with my patients."

The response I got was less than unsatisfying—the bureaucratic equivalent of a blank stare. The new administrator was absolutely terrified to take a stand or risk making enemies, even in the face of what seemed to me like overwhelming evidence of Dr. Morelli's corrupt and dangerous behavior. The CEO was unwilling to listen to reason and take steps to protect patients.

I had no choice, so I told Canyon Meadows, "That's it. I'm moving all my patients to BCMC." And that's exactly what I did. I took the patient with bladder cancer, whose operation Dr. Morelli and Singh had canceled, and transferred him to BCMC, where I performed the orthotopic neobladder procedure without any problem.

Immediately, the spotlight that had shone on me at Canyon Meadows began to glow at BCMC. The patients I had been treating followed me, and new patients came as well, bringing revenue in with them. The administrators at BCMC loved me. I had been working there from time to time for months, consulting on cases and bringing patients there when no beds or operating rooms were available at Canyon Meadows. They knew exactly what kind of surgeon I was, and they were determined to make me as happy as possible and allow me to do the kind of high-quality work that would reflect well on them and attract patients.

At Canyon Meadows, Dr. Morelli's reign of terror continued and in fact seemed to get even worse. But their revenue took a serious hit without me there to bring in rich people needing the kind of difficult operations I was now performing at BCMC. Before long they were laying people off, and I started getting phone calls from members of the board of trustees and doctors.

"Please, you've got to come back," I was told. They were verging on panic.

"I'm not coming anywhere near that place," I said. "Not with that malignant son of a bitch in the building. I'm not gonna be in the same hospital with that guy." It wasn't just about our personal feud; as long as Dr. Morelli's presence was tolerated, Canyon Meadows was not somewhere I could safely bring patients. The fact that they had allowed him to practice for so long, in the face of all the evidence of his malpractice and misconduct, showed them to be an institution that would need serious help if they were ever going to recover their reputation.

At some point, they must have realized this themselves, because the Canyon Meadows administration finally made the decision to rid themselves of him, and they did so in an aggressive and publicly humiliating manner.

Taking into account his long-established and well-earned reputation for violence, they called the local police before informing him that he was being terminated. They fired him as chief of surgery, and he was escorted off the grounds at Canyon Meadows Medical Center by the police. He was told by the hospital's parent company, Careline Health, that he was never to set foot on any of their properties again. They had two hospitals in the area, Canyon Meadows and Lake Regional Medical Center in Lake Havasu, Arizona, where I also had staff privileges. One of the board of trustees members called me and said, "Dr. Panvini, we got rid of the cancer, and we need you back here!"

For a brief moment, it felt like a victory. Dr. Morelli, who was a genuine danger to patients and a horrible person to work with, had been stripped of his authority and banished from the hospital. But what happened next was possibly more shocking. With no place else to go, he went to BCMC—and they took him on!

Olivia, BCMC's head nurse, and I had been working together, and we nearly fell over when we heard the news. We immediately decided that it was time to go, and she relocated to the Midwest.

Fortunately Canyon Meadows' board of trustees was already making overtures to me. I was contacted almost as soon as he was fired. "Dr. Panvini," I was told, "You have been a valued member of our staff, and we want you back very badly." They offered me the position of chairman of surgery at Canyon Meadows, holding an election and voting unanimously to bring me on board. Upon my return, I quickly realized that there was a tremendous amount of work to be done to clean up the mess Dr. Morelli had left behind. It was almost as if he had intentionally planted land mines that would explode when the hospital went through reaccreditation. He had removed all of the protocols for procedures in the operating room and destroyed the minutes of the surgical meetings for the past year, and he left a generally toxic environment. And there was much more.

CHAPTER TWENTY-FIVE

A Committee Like No Other

Dr. Morelli had made such a mess of Canyon Meadows Medical Center during his time as chief of surgery that the hospital was in danger of losing its accreditation. Hospitals across the United States are accredited by the Joint Commission, formerly known as the Joint Commission on Accreditation of Healthcare Organizations, an independent, not-for-profit organization. Joint Commission accreditation and certification is recognized throughout the health care field as an honest reflection of a hospital's commitment to quality and performance standards.

After years of Morelli's misconduct and incompetence, the surgical department was so far out of whack that I was forced to restructure the organization to get it running the way it needed to be.

Problem solving is one of my attributes. When I'm faced with a difficult problem, I meditate and visualize all of the factors involved in my analysis. It's like making sure the pieces of a puzzle fit together perfectly. I have to mold my mind and fully grasp the problem before I come up with a solution. First I analyzed all of the issues that needed to be addressed and came up with a common denominator, which was communication. Then I sat down with every department head and asked them what they thought needed to be fixed. Finally I took all of that essential input under consideration before developing my final course of action.

I decided that clear lines of communication would be vitally important moving forward, and I drew on my experience at BCMC, where I had chaired the operating room safety committee. I formed what I called the OR Patient Safety Committee, which included representatives from every department at the hospital—from the CEO to administration to purchasing to maintenance to the nursing staff, the surgical staff, the pathology department, the radiology department, and down the list.

As I said earlier, hospitals are complex organizations, and a problem for one department can quickly become a problem for others, and ultimately for everyone. My solution was to bring everyone together to respond to issues as soon as they arose. This would ensure that everyone had a voice and that good ideas would be accepted, no matter where they came from. It would also make the system work faster, because we wouldn't have to wait for issues to arise and be handled by one committee before being passed along to another; we could have an open forum discussion with everyone together in one room.

It wasn't long before a serious situation arose. Dr. Paul Assad, a vascular surgeon on staff, had performed an operation to repair an abdominal aortic aneurysm—what's known as an AAA—on a patient. The abdominal aorta is a major vessel that supplies blood to the body's legs and organs; an aneurysm occurs when the vessel's wall weakens and begins to swell outward. The procedure involves opening the patient's abdomen and sewing a prosthetic graft into the aorta, to get rid of the bulging and permit healthy blood flow to the legs.

Dr. Assad called me during the procedure and said, "Dr. Panvini, I'm just closing up this patient, and we have a discrepancy in the lap pad count."

A laparotomy pad is a small absorbent cloth towel, with a radiographic wire that can be seen on X-rays, that's used to pack off organs and keep things out of the way while an operation is in progress. The pads are white and have a blue tag sewn on the corner, extending along one edge. When a surgical team finishes an operation, they carefully count everything used during the course of the procedure, to make sure nothing has been left inside the patient's body. If a lap pad was missing, it was almost certainly tucked away inside the patient's abdomen and needed to be retrieved.

"Did you check the retroperitoneum?" I asked, referring to an area behind the aorta. As a urologist, I was required to do two years of general surgery; I had been on this type of case many times.

"Let me check," he replied.

I asked, "What did the X-ray show?" Patients are x-rayed after operations to see if anything has been left behind.

He told me the X-rays were clear, but I told him to have the nurses run another one, just to be sure.

He called me back after the second set of X-rays was run. They didn't show anything, but there was still a discrepancy in the count; two lap pads were missing. We decided to close up the patient.

A few weeks later, the patient was admitted to BCMC. Wes Brown, the surgeon operating on him, called me to ask if I had any knowledge of the patient, since he had been at Canyon Meadows first. When I acknowledged that I did, Wes asked me to tell him whatever I could.

"Do me a favor, Wes," I said. "Give the guy a CAT scan and call me back."

When we spoke again, he told me the CAT scan was negative; it showed nothing unusual.

I told him, "Listen, Wes, there was a lap pad discrepancy with this patient. I suggest you reexplore him and see if you find anything. I would pay particular attention to the retroperitoneum, but I'm just a urologist. You're the surgeon."

After opening the patient up, Brown contacted me again. He had found two lap pads in the man's abdominal cavity, tucked away out of sight in the retroperitoneum.

I knew this meant trouble, because we were at risk for a major lawsuit. I said, "Wes, I want those pads sequestered. Take X-rays of them, and then please send them over to Canyon Meadows. We're going to have a meeting about this case today."

We got the X-rays from BCMC, and they showed no evidence of any radiographic markers. I was astonished. How could this be? Lap pads were supposed to contain radiographic markers, small wires of metallic material that were easy for an X-ray machine to spot.

In the OR Safety Committee Meeting at Canyon Meadows, with all departments present, I had Dr. Assad recount the story of the operation from beginning to end. Then the nurses gave their perspective. After they spoke, while the rest of the departments were talking, I asked the nurses to go into the hospital's stockroom and get samples of lap pads from every month for the past year, take X-rays of them, and bring the X-rays to the meeting. They did so.

The radiologist read the X-rays in the meeting, with everyone else looking on. About four months before Dr.

Assad's operation, the lap pads had ceased to contain radiographic markers.

I looked at the administration's representative on the committee and asked, "What did you do differently starting in May 2012?"

They tossed the question to the purchasing rep, who said, "We started buying them from a Chinese company."

"Why?" I asked.

"They quoted us a better discount than American companies could provide."

I said, "Well, I think I can see why. Until that month, all the lap pads had radiographic markers, and as soon as you began using the ones supplied by this Chinese company, there were no more markers. This is a patient safety issue, and it needs to be resolved right away."

I laid out new protocols to cope with the materials we had on hand, including the use of CAT scans as an additional way to make sure nothing was left inside patients. Then I rendered my judgment on the incident: "I see no issues with what was done by the surgeon, nursing staff, administration, or purchasing department. The blame falls on the Chinese company from whom we purchased these lap pads." With that, I gaveled the meeting to a close.

As soon as I did so, everyone in the room rose and gave me a standing ovation. I had saved several employees' jobs and avoided a major potential lawsuit. We had reached a solution in a single meeting, determining the exact nature of the problem and instituting a preventive measure. The system was working exactly as I had hoped.

Soon after that, representatives from the Joint Commission came in to inspect Canyon Meadows and went through the entire hospital thoroughly. I had cleaned up as much as I could, and I didn't foresee any problems. But when I got a call from administration telling me that the people from the Joint Commission wanted to meet with me, I was nervous.

I said, "Okay, have them come over to my office." I was in the middle of a busy day, seeing a bunch of patients, when they showed up. They all had the same haircut and were wearing black suits, white shirts, and black ties, just like in the *Men in Black* movie.

When I came out of one of the exam rooms and saw them all sitting silently in my office, I started shaking slightly. As calmly as possible, I said, "I'm Dr. Panvini, chief of surgery. Nice to meet you."

They stood and gave me their names, which I was too nervous to remember.

I asked, "What can I do for you?"

One of them said, "Dr. Panvini, as we've gone through your hospital for reaccreditation, we have come across some enlightening issues."

Remaining silent, I thought, *Oh my God, what the hell's going on now?*

He continued, "After reading the minutes from your OR Patient Safety Committee meeting, we wanted to tell you that in all the years that we've been in the field, we've never seen a committee so innovative, dynamic, and quick to come to a resolution."

I was shocked. The Joint Commission had been doing this work for something like twenty-five years.

He said the minutes from the previous month's meeting read like a Michael Crichton novel. "We want you to know that for establishing that committee, you'll be receiving an award from JCAHO."

I tried to stay calm and joked, "Oh, okay, but my hat isn't gonna fit now."

"We also want you to know that because of the formation of this committee, Careline Health will also be receiving an award from JCAHO. Of course, the accreditation standards have been met as well; you're going to be reaccredited because we have not been able to find any violations."

I thanked them profusely. It was quite flattering. They continued to praise me and Canyon Meadows, saying that in their entire history in the field, they had never seen a committee of that nature. Canyon Meadows's OR Patient Safety Committee was going to be emulated in every hospital throughout the country, and they considered it to be the most dynamic committee they had ever encountered and exactly what they were looking for.

Finally, they all shook my hand and left, and I went back to seeing patients. An hour or so later, I got a page summoning me to the board meeting room immediately. Like before, I said to myself, *Oh shit, what the hell happened now?*

I told my staff, "You need to reschedule my patients. I have to go to an emergency administrative meeting." As I walked next door to the hospital, I was wondering what I had missed that would warrant reaccreditation concerns. Approaching the boardroom, I didn't see anybody in the corridor outside. I opened the door, but the room was dark so I turned on the light. There were people from every Canyon Meadows department, with bottles of champagne that they sprayed all over me in celebration.

That was the highest point of my career in a lot of ways. I was really proud to have that kind of effect on a huge organization like Canyon Meadows, and to know that going forward, patients would be safer and the system would be more efficient. Needless to say, the hospital was always in excellent standing after that.

CHAPTER TWENTY-SIX

Things Are Not What They Seem

When I was forced to leave Nevada in 2010, after being accused by my ex-wife of being a drug addict and suffering a spinal injury that nearly left me permanently paralyzed, I had to close my office in a hurry. In fact, I had been forced to rely on my staff to handle the logistical issues for me, since I was immobilized in a hospital bed.

More than a year later, I was doing much better. I had managed to escape the malignant influence of Dr. Morelli, and I was winning awards for my work at Canyon Meadows Medical Center. I was building a successful practice in a new state, and things really seemed to be looking up. Unfortunately, my creditors were beginning to circle like sharks.

The company from which I had rented office space in Nevada filed a $250,000 lawsuit against me for breaking my lease—and they weren't the only people to whom I owed money. When I reestablished myself in Arizona, I had borrowed close to a million dollars from friends and relatives to set up my office, hire new staff, and purchase the equipment and materials that would allow me to do my work. I had also borrowed $400,000 from Northern Nevada Medical Center, though that debt was later forgiven after I worked there for a contractually agreed upon length of time.

Under pressure to repay these debts, I was doing so as fast as I could, but eventually it all reached a crisis point. My former landlord in Nevada had filed his lawsuit, and my ex-wife was swooping in again like a vulture. She had raised a fraudulent issue about child support, including a phony warrant for my arrest, and she was doing everything she could to destroy my reputation, as usual. But that was put to rest by the prosecutor in Indiana eventually.

Then the worst possible thing happened—something that even I could not have predicted. Chelsea partnered up with the Morellis and they began pursuing me together, even luring Natasha over to their side. She, in turn, divulged this information to my father, which is how I found out about the collusion. Dr. Morelli told my daughter that I was a thief and a criminal, and that I was going to jail for the rest of my life. I hadn't seen Natasha since the divorce papers were filed, and Chelsea had of course been poisoning her against me all along. Hearing something like that was sure to make our already strained relationship even worse.

Before long, I could barely see a way out from under my mountains of debt. I wasn't humanly capable of seeing enough patients or working enough hours to make up the difference. Finally I said to myself, *I'm buried, so I'll just make a fresh start.* I decided to file for bankruptcy, with the intent of freeing myself from my business debts, but also discharging what I owed Chelsea. I knew that had been improperly determined in the first place, because the court had miscalculated my income. They wanted me to pay her a totally unreasonable amount of money in settlement and child support, without taking into account the damage she had done to my earning potential. My attorney at the time assured me that this was possible.

Meanwhile I also had a legal action in process against Dr. Morelli. He had filed a lawsuit against me, charging me with defamation of character because of all the things I had revealed about his shoddy and dangerous medical practices. His lawsuit would never have gone anywhere, because when you file a qui tam lawsuit, you have immunity. But when I filed for bankruptcy, he brought our conflicts with his lawsuit into the bankruptcy proceeding, making himself a creditor and turning the whole thing into a three-ring circus. He had obviously been informed by my ex-wife that I was filing for bankruptcy, since she was a creditor.

Teamed up with my ex-wife and daughter, Morelli and his wife attempted to involve the police and raised legal conflicts from other states. They apparently tried to contact everyone I had ever known, trying to dig up dirt and damage my reputation. They contacted my colleagues, mother and father, sisters, friends, and other relatives—even my best friend, Doug, from New York.

One of my lawyers provided me with this message:

> Comments: Dear Attorney Gorsky, Dr. Dino Panvini has listed you as a creditor in his bankruptcy petition for $5,000. He has also listed my husband who has a civil suit pending against Dr. Panvini. As I go through Dr. Panvini's petition, I am finding some inconsistencies. If this amount is incorrect or does not exist, I was wondering if you could email the trustee at glopinsky@7trustee.net. Thank you for your time. Margaret Morelli.

He responded to her:

> Dear Ms. Morelli, I will not be able to respond to your question. In my view the question you pose, if answered, would violate the privilege that exists between a lawyer and his client. Alan Gorsky, Esq.

These people all notified me about these issues. I know that this was all based on information they had received from Chelsea, because she knew who my friends were. They were painting a picture of me, for the court and people who knew me, as a criminal who was headed to jail.

The Morellis charged me with bankruptcy fraud and accused me of being a fugitive from the state of Indiana. During the questioning, Margaret Morelli asked me if I owned a handgun. I said that I did, and that it was kept at my house. She asked this at the meeting of the creditors and Connor Truman, my ex-wife's lawyer, with whom the Morellis had aligned themselves. I lived within Native American tribal territory, and under federal law, Native Americans who live on a reservation aren't allowed to own handguns. But guns are perfectly legal for other Americans who live there, especially with a permit for a concealed weapon (CCW). In fact, 95 percent of non–Native Americans who live on tribal territory own weapons.

But the Morellis twisted things around so crazily that in the middle of the night, the police knocked on my door. They then proceeded to ransack my entire house, turning everything upside down.

I asked, "What are you looking for?"

"A gun," they said.

"I'll show you the gun, and my CCW too." When I did so, they confiscated the gun, which they claimed that I wasn't allowed to have, and handed me a summons.

The charges were filed by the tribal police in Mohave County. Speaking later with Richard Yella, the tribal police chief, I learned that he was best friends with the Morellis and often had dinner with them. Also, Margaret Morelli was working as an unpaid pseudo-paralegal for Connor Truman. When I asked the chief to drop the charges, he refused to do so.

I later consulted several judges and verified that the law applies only to Native Americans living on tribal land, not to other American citizens. Furthermore, it's a hundred-year-old law from the era when cowboys and Indians were making peace treaties. It had nothing to do with my rights as an American citizen, especially since I had a CCW. My constitutional rights as an American citizen were violated by the Mohave tribal police. This all happened in 2013 after Dr. Morelli was kicked out of the hospital.

The Nevada medical board began to make inquiries about this, and I had no choice but to respond. Somehow Truman and the Morellis knew someone on the Nevada board, and the board sanctioned me for being fined by the tribal police for having a handgun, despite the fact that I had a CCW. Then they began telling people that I had been arrested for illegal possession of a firearm, spreading these rumors to my referring doctors. It had the desired effect; little by little, other doctors started to have questions about me, and some of them never even contacted me to find out the truth. Dr. Morelli and his wife were strategically trying to drive me out of town.

The Morellis even filed a complaint against me with the Department of Health and Human Services, alleging that I had improperly disclosed patients' private medical information. Meanwhile *they* were trying to get their hands on *my* private medical information and use it against me. My attorney, who wasn't as intelligent as I needed him to be, tried to look up the relevant HIPAA laws, as though there was some circumstance in which my medical files could be released to those people.

"Listen," I told him, "my private health care information is not public information. It's protected by federal laws through the Department of Health and Human Services. Don't you understand that, you idiot?"

He responded that he needed to look up these laws because he wasn't familiar with them. At times I felt like I was teaching my lawyer how to do his job.

In June 2013, I traveled to Italy to give a lecture with my father, who was disabled, living as an amputee in a wheelchair, and requiring oxygen to breathe through his tracheostomy. We gave a lecture on various hernia topics, and I gave a presentation in Caserta on the latest trends and laser prostatectomies. As we were returning to the United States, a Customs officer detained us for something that I still can't understand to this day. It was obvious that Dr. Morelli had used his father's influence as a federal attorney and pulled some strings to make my life miserable.

My father went into a rage, and I thought he was going to have a heart attack. I told him, "Please calm down. We'll get to the bottom of this."

Then I explained to the Customs officer that there were people who were making fraudulent claims about me. He looked on his computer screen and verified what I was telling him. I was confused about what he was reading, but after laborious discussion, he realized that whatever was on the screen didn't make any sense, even though I had somehow been flagged by Customs. Nonetheless, the Customs officers ransacked our luggage, apparently looking for drugs. Of course they found nothing, and after having been detained for hours, we were released.

My father and I were both furious. That's when he really understood what I was going through and the hardships being imposed on me by my ex-wife. Also during that trip to Italy, it finally sank in that my attorney was totally incompetent. So I fired him and hired another law firm, Hanson, Lawson & Kaplan. What happened next convinced me that they, too, had been paid off or were in the pocket of the Morellis.

I told my new attorneys, "I am being hassled on a daily basis with fraudulent claims, which has interfered with every aspect of my life. You need to do something about these constant interruptions and conclude this bankruptcy issue once and for all."

I explained what I wanted to accomplish, and they confidently assured me, "Yeah, we can take care of this." Not long afterward, though, they informed me that my payments to my ex-wife weren't dischargeable in bankruptcy court.

I said, "What? My other lawyer told me it could be done."

"Well, he was wrong," they said. So I had to abandon my hope of discharging those payments, removed that from the bankruptcy suit, and focused on all my other debts.

Meanwhile, the bankruptcy court proceedings were becoming more bizarre, as Dr. Morelli and his wife threw one thing after another at me. It was becoming a truly humiliating spectacle. The low point was when Margaret attended a meeting of creditors with one of my former patients, Emily Pitt, in tow! She was representing Dr. Morelli as his wife, contesting that I had filed a fraudulent legal action with the federal government that injured Dr. Morelli's reputation. So at the meeting of the creditors, Margaret was given the opportunity to ask questions, in collusion with Connor Truman, my ex-wife's attorney.

I had treated Emily Pitt for invasive bladder cancer, and without surgery, she would have died. I had offered to surgically remove her cancer and construct an orthotopic neobladder, using the procedure I described earlier. Shortly after I operated on her, she came back to the office to tell me that she was extremely appreciative of everything I had done for her. I had given her "a whole new life," in her words. She had lost weight, which improved her self-image, and I had even cured a problem with her gait, because she had been suffering a linoleic acid deficiency that interfered with the conduction of nerve impulses and made walking difficult.

In the office that day, she gave me a card. Extremely busy, I quickly thanked her, saying, "You didn't have to do that." Then I slipped the card into my desk and thought nothing more of it.

About two weeks later, I was in the middle of a typically busy day, seeing patients one after another. Then Betty, who managed my OR schedule, came in to tell me that Emily Pitt was in the office ... and she wanted her key back.

Key? What key?

"The key that was in the card she gave you," Betty said.

When I thought back to her previous visit, I remembered that I'd put the card somewhere in my desk. With Betty's help, I found it at the bottom of a drawer. The card said, "To my knight in shining armor," and below that Emily had written her address, the kind of cars she owned, and her phone number. And sure enough, there was a house key tucked inside the card.

I almost laughed out loud. Turning to Betty, I asked, "Can you believe this?" She was as shocked as I was.

This kind of thing happens with doctors a lot—patients develop unhealthy fixations. It's something you always have to be on guard against, and of course you have to behave in a morally correct fashion and never exploit your position. Stories about doctors sexually abusing their patients always make me sad, not only for the people involved, but also because they drag down the entire medical profession. As I've said, we Panvini's have been doctors for centuries, and it's more than a job for me; it's a calling.

I told Betty, "I want you to scan this immediately and put it in the EMR. Then leave the card in her chart, but give her key back." She did, and Emily left.

Months later, the Morellis and Connor Truman, working with Veronica Fischer, were using Emily Pitt as a pawn. They made false allegations to the Arizona medical licensing board that I had molested her and had been having an affair with her.

The allegations were easily disproved because my nurse, Susan, was always present with me and Emily Pitt. Susan was fascinated by the surgeries that I performed, and she always asked questions and paid attention to how our patients were following up.

When we got to the hearing, the board examiner asked Susan and me a series of questions. He also had a binder full of documents, provided by my lawyer, proving that the allegations were fraudulent.

The board examiner asked me, "When you examined Mrs. Pitt, what exactly were you looking for?"

I answered that I had done a neobladder on her, so I was assessing for postoperative incontinence.

"And when you examined for incontinence, exactly what did you do?"

I responded that I have the patient lie in the lithotomy position. Then I open the labia with my left hand as I shield myself with my right hand, being gloved for stress incontinence, and ask her to cough.

The examiner asked, "Where is your nurse at this time?"

I answered, "She is beside my right hand, just behind me, at all times."

"Was there anything inappropriate about your examination of the patient?"

"Absolutely not," I said. "The findings were that she had some mild stress incontinence that needed to be addressed with a mini sling."

Then the examiner asked my nurse, "Were you present when Dr. Panvini examined Emily Pitt?"

Susan answered, "I'm always present with Dr. Panvini and every patient whom he examines, especially women. Yes, I was present at all times while Emily Pitt was being examined."

"Was there anything abnormal during Dr. Panvini's evaluation?"

"No, nothing outside of the finding that she was incontinent when she coughed, which is normal after this type of procedure."

"So are you asserting that Emily Pitt is lying when she claims that she was molested by Dr. Panvini?"

"Absolutely," Susan replied. "Dr. Panvini never did anything inappropriate to Emily Pitt during his evaluation, and I was present during every visit. Can I show you the card?"

The examiner asked, "What card?"

With an obvious sense of excitement and pride, Susan opened the binder right to the card and showed the examiner what Emily had written there. "You see," Susan explained, "this patient is crazy. She was infatuated with my Dr. Panvini."

The examiner read the card and said, "Wow. Okay, I think this answers the question."

So when Truman and Emily Pitt made her complaint to the Arizona medical licensing board that I had molested her, I went down there with Susan and my attorney, William Condor, and we cleared up all the allegations in a single meeting. Once we showed them the card, the charge was dismissed with prejudice against Emily Pitt.

I knew there was nothing to it, but a lot of doctors have lost their licenses because of fraudulent allegations. I didn't realize until then just how deeply Emily was connected to Dr. Morelli. When Margaret and Truman brought her to the creditors' meeting, I thought, *Okay, the gloves are off.*

That wasn't the last time I would hear from Emily. Once she connected with Connor Truman, the story took an entirely new turn. She then filed a malpractice action against me on the basis of her having suffered some mild incontinence after I constructed her new bladder, under the guidance of Truman. Of course, I had informed her that this was a potential side effect from the beginning. In fact, I had planned to construct a pelvic sling for her, which would have resolved the issue. However, when she displayed affection toward me by giving me the card and her house key, I was forced to stop seeing her as a patient. To avoid even the appearance of impropriety, I had told her to find another doctor. The doctor she chose performed the mini-sling procedure, and her incontinence was resolved.

I first encountered Connor Truman when he was representing Chelsea at the meeting with my creditors. He was a tall, obese man with dark brown hair and a sarcastic attitude. Mind you, he was a bankruptcy attorney trying to act as a malpractice attorney. I was still trying to sort out the bankruptcy and eliminate the payments to my ex-wife, and they were there to make that impossible.

Then Truman aligned himself with the Morellis, and they all went after me like vultures. He hired Margaret as a professional expert witness against me, despite the fact that she had neither legal nor medical expertise. She had never worked in an operating room, and she had never even worked in a hospital; she had been in her husband's office, and that was it.

I was ultimately able to prevail against Emily Pitt. Her case was dismissed with prejudice against her a year after it was submitted in 2014. There was no proof to support any of her allegations, but substantial evidence that she had been infatuated with me. I was also able to settle some matters with the Morellis, although I can't say much about that since it has been sealed by the court. We did reach an agreement that he and I would dismiss our actions against each other and never cross paths again.

I had simply had enough, so I said to my attorney, "Listen, you gotta do something to get rid of this parasite." He was able to reach an agreement with the Morellis that included a settlement, and I agreed not to practice in that area for three years. Even then, however, I was betrayed, because the three years turned into ten years. Looking back now, I suspect that my ex-attorney was on the other side, because I wasn't part of that decision while I was in Italy in 2014.

With the Morellis out of the way, I was able to finish my bankruptcy filing. That should have been the end of the matter, and I should have been able to move on with my life then, but Truman wasn't finished yet. His biggest mistake, which would rebound against him later, was to continue pursuing me after Emily Pitt's case fell apart. He found another client and came after me again, and again, and again. In the end, relentless pursuit would prove to be his undoing.

CHAPTER TWENTY-SEVEN

Fraudulent Malpractice

Albert Marin was an eighty-one-year-old man with health problems. When he was referred to me, in my position at Canyon Meadows Medical Center, by a doctor named Wilek, I did a workup on him and found that he had cancer in his left kidney. It was a serious issue, so I sat down with him immediately.

"Listen," I said, "you have cancer of the kidney. I consider it malignant until proven otherwise, and I'm going to offer you some options. Because of your age, you always have the option to just wait and watch, but that will require ancillary tests and the possibility of getting MRIs and CT scans every couple of months, to monitor the growth of the mass. The problem is that if the mass does start to grow and metastasize, it will be too late—there will be no cure. However, we can also perform either laparoscopic or open surgery to remove it."

I also explained that there were other procedures that I refused to do, such as cryoablation and radiofrequency ablation. Cryoablation involves inserting a fine needle through the skin into the target site and delivering argon gas under pressure to the tip of the needle, where it cools to an extremely cold temperature to freeze and kill the tumor. Radiofrequency ablation is similar, but the surgeon uses an electrode rather than a frozen needle to basically zap the tumor. Unfortunately there's a risk that these treatments won't destroy all of the cancerous tissue. They might even spread it along the tract, which means the disease could return. Because of that risk, I was not an advocate of either of these procedures.

I told Mr. Marin, "If you want either of those procedures done, go someplace else, because I'm not gonna do it. I'll send you to California for that."

He replied, "No, I just want the cancer out. I don't want to have anything in my body and have to worry about it later on." Ultimately, Mr. Marin elected to have the surgical nephrectomy.

Before I removed his left kidney, he needed a separate procedure to break up some kidney stones. Once that was accomplished, I performed the primary procedure laparoscopically on September 24, 2012. This entailed creating a small puncture wound through the umbilicus and a small incision, where my hand went through a GelPort. This procedure is called a hand-assisted laparoscopic nephrectomy (HAL). The operation went as close to perfectly as it could have gone. He might have lost a hundred ccs of blood, which is nothing for a nephrectomy. Overall, the procedure was uneventful and I got the cancer out completely. Mr. Marin went back to the recovery room and then to the ICU.

The next day, though, Mr. Marin couldn't move his legs. And when I felt his feet, they were ice cold, something that the nurse, Doug Meadows, had never checked. Mr. Marin had also developed anuria, which meant that his remaining kidney was not producing urine. That was serious and required immediate attention, so I called in several other specialists to consult, including a vascular surgeon. A renal scan showed that the patient had a blockage to his right kidney, which meant he needed an aortogram, dialysis, and a bypass. It was obvious that Mr. Marin needed a higher level of care than Canyon Meadows Medical Center was prepared to provide, so I had him transferred to Sunrise Medical Center in Las Vegas, a process that took several hours.

When they operated on him at Sunrise, they found that the arteries leading to his spinal cord, his right kidney, and apparently all the way down the lower half of his body were badly blocked because of atherosclerosis. He also suffered from amyloidosis, which was not known preoperatively, in which a protein called amyloid, normally present in bone marrow, filters into other parts of the body, ultimately causing organ failure. Mr. Marin remained hospitalized and eventually died on September 27, ten days after I had operated on him.

I believe that Doug Meadows was working with Dr. Morelli, because Doug immediately started to spread rumors that I had done something wrong. Morelli and Connor Truman accused me of medical malpractice, claiming that Mr. Marin's death was my fault. They slithered up to his grieving widow and convinced her that I had killed him. Perhaps the worst part, though, was that they didn't even tell her what they were accusing me of doing!

In a deposition conducted by my attorney, Caleb Wilder, he revealed to Mrs. Marin that Truman's complaint read, in part, "Mr. Marin's artery was damaged as a result of Dr. Panvini's surgery, causing a complete loss of blood flow to the right kidney and paralysis to his lower extremities, eventually leading to his untimely death."

They were claiming that I had tied off his abdominal aorta and then closed him up with it in that condition, depriving his lower extremities of blood. This was impossible, because the abdominal aorta is one of the largest blood vessels in the human body. The size of your wrist, it carries blood to all the lower extremities. And in a patient with atherosclerosis, like Mr. Marin, it can't be sutured or sealed off, because the vessel itself has hardened to the point that trying to tie it shut would be like wrapping a rubber band around a PVC pipe and expecting it to close.

I had performed that surgery with the utmost care and thought. I had brought in special instruments for him, because I knew he had atherosclerosis of the renal artery. I had chosen to use a manual Covidien stapler to close off his blood vessels, rather than the Ethicon stapler, which is less effective in this case. The stapler I chose is used by thoracic surgeons to handle the trachea and the bronchial tubes, which are made of tough cartilage.

But the complaint didn't just allege that I was a bad doctor; they claimed that my actions were deliberate. Truman had also written that "Dr. Panvini, knowing full well that he had made an error in the surgery of Mr. Marin, made a decision not to fix the error and instead concluded the surgery." When he said I "made a decision," he was in effect accusing me of murder.

The full list of charges included the assertions that I lacked the experience to perform a laparoscopic nephrectomy; that I had misrepresented my knowledge and skills to the Marins; and that I had made an error during surgery, closed Mr. Marin up without solving the problem, hidden that from everyone, and then delayed his transfer to Sunrise—sending him by ambulance rather than by helicopter—to cover up my incompetence, even while knowing it would probably kill him.

My attorney, Caleb Wilder, who knew Truman, actually tried to offer him a way out of the peril in which he was placing himself. He sent Truman a letter to inform him that he was at risk of violating Rule 11, which states in part that attorneys must not file lawsuits or bring charges without possessing evidence to support the allegations contained in the complaints.

Truman didn't care. He had absolutely no case, but he refused to let it go. He made wild, reckless charges and then took his case from venue to venue in a vain attempt to find a judge who would grant him the verdict and damages that he sought. He failed in federal court in Nevada, and then in state court in Arizona. There was no evidence to substantiate their claims, so when the case was brought to the judge's bench, it was dismissed with prejudice against them.

Finally, in June 2014, Truman filed the case in Arizona Federal District Court. By then, I had closed my office and left for Italy. My lawyer informed Truman of those circumstances, asking him why he was suing a company that no longer existed and how he intended to serve me with legal papers:

> Finally, you previously promised that before any attempt to renew litigation against Dr. Panvini (and I never stipulated that you would have the legal ability to do this), you would first provide me with expert medical opinions to support your allegation that Dr. Panvini was negligent and that such negligence caused the death of Mr. Marin. You have not done so, and once again all you have presented are unsupported allegations and conclusory statements ... As I

have been asking you for well over a year, if you have the evidence, then please present it.

The following letter, prepared by my malpractice attorney Caleb Wilder, describes the sequence of Truman's charges against me:

> Ostensibly, the litigation all stems from a laparoscopic nephrectomy performed by Dr. Panvini on Mr. Marin at The Medical Center on September 24, 2012. Mr. Marin, an eighty-one-year-old man, had a suspicious mass on his left kidney which was proven to be renal cell carcinoma. Although the surgery was technically difficult due a large amount of aberrant vessels, it was performed without complications and the blood loss was extremely minimal.
>
> Following surgery Mr. Marin was evaluated by a physician and a number of nurses in the PACU, all of whom found that Mr. Marin was able to feel and move his legs. However, several hours later Mr. Marin lost sensation and movement in his legs. This was initially felt to be secondary to epidural anesthesia. However, after discontinuation of the epidural and imaging studies, it was determined that Mr. Marin had developed a post-operative occlusion of the abdominal aorta. Upon receiving this information, you immediately initiated a

transfer to Sunrise Medical Center in Las Vegas. Following his arrival at Sunrise, Mr. Marin was taken into surgery where a bilateral aorto-femoral bypass was performed. Notably the surgeon reported absolutely no injury or trauma to the aorta; rather, it was felt that Mr. Marin's severe and extensive atherosclerosis was to blame for the aortic occlusion. Unfortunately, Mr. Marin died several days later; the autopsy once again confirmed the lack of injury or trauma to the abdominal aorta.

After these events, for your own personal reason, you filed bankruptcy in Nevada, where you were living at the time. Connor Truman, Esq., a Las Vegas bankruptcy attorney, became involved in the case because he represented your ex-wife as well as a number of other creditors. In addition, Mr. Truman, who candidly admits that he knows nothing about medicine, somehow persuaded Mr. Marin's widow to sue you and to allow him to do so as part of the bankruptcy proceeding. He filed a medical malpractice lawsuit in bankruptcy court.

Several months later Mr. Truman did a despicable thing. He amended his complaint to drop the negligence claims and to allege that you *intentionally* caused the death of Mr. Marin.

Specifically, he accused you of purposefully "tying off" the abdominal aorta, ending the case knowing that you had done this, and then lying about it afterward in an attempt to cover up your act, the equivalent of murder.

I was stunned and immediately contacted Mr. Truman to demand an explanation for why he had done this and for specific evidence to support his outlandish claims. Mr. Truman freely admitted that he had *no* evidence and *no* basis for his claims. Amazingly, he also admitted that the only reason he was making these "intentional act" claims was that he hoped to reach your personal assets (*i.e.* disallow your bankruptcy protection) *and* to collect under your insurance policy. Mr. Truman also admitted that he felt that this ploy would save him some money, as it would somehow allow him to compel you to return to the United States from Italy for your deposition, thus eliminating the need for him to travel to Italy. I repeatedly tried to explain to Mr. Truman that his actions were unethical, immoral, and made no sense legally. Mr. Truman responded by agreeing that his tactics were not fair to you, but he felt that it was the best way to get what he wanted. I made it very clear to Mr. Truman that I was in complete disagreement with his thinking and that I would have no problem testifying in the future that I felt he was committing severe ethical violations, ignoring clear conflicts of interest, and committing legal malpractice. I repeatedly urged Mr. Truman to withdraw these intentional act claims and to revert back to his initial negligence claims, but he refused to do so.

Keeping up the pressure, I served discovery requests demanding evidence to support these claims. Mr. Truman produced nothing. I deposed Mrs. Marin, and she admitted that she had no idea whether any of these allegations were true, and confirmed that she was relying on Mr. Truman to prove them. Eventually, I had a basis to move for sanctions due to Mr. Truman's failure to produce any evidence, and on the eve of the hearing, Mr. Truman finally agreed to stipulate to withdraw the intentional act claims.

You subsequently filed an abuse of process lawsuit against Mr. Truman and Mrs. Marin.

As I told you previously, this was the first time in my twenty-five years of practice that I have felt that a physician was justified in suing a plaintiff attorney. It is my understanding that the lawsuit is ongoing, and I wish you great success in it.

Several months passed, and just before the running out of the statute of limitations, Mr. Truman filed a new medical malpractice lawsuit against you. That lawsuit is ongoing and I am proud to represent you in this. Mr. Truman has yet to produce any evidence of what you supposedly did wrong during this surgery, and in contrast we have assembled a strong team of experts who are confident that you met the standard of care in all respects and that you are in no way responsible for the death of Mr. Marin. I am totally confident that the jury will agree that you are not liable and I look forward to your vindication at trial.

Sincerely,

Caleb Wilder

It was like Truman couldn't stop himself. He proceeded to federal court with no more evidence than he'd presented in any previous iteration of the case. He was like a child who believes that saying the same thing over and over magically makes it true—but it *wasn't* true. Obviously these actions were for secondary gains. A forensic pathologist evaluated the case and discovered that Mr. Marin had amyloidosis. Nobody had any knowledge of his condition before that, because it wasn't something for which anyone had screened. He had also suffered a heart attack in the hospital, as it turned out.

I won the case against Truman, once and for all, on October 17, 2017, in Arizona Federal Court. The result was an 8-0 vote in my favor.

His arguments would have been laughable had they not presented such a danger to me and my career. As I was in the court watching these proceedings, it was like watching a television sitcom. He presented witnesses who had no direct knowledge of the case in question, but who were just there to impugn my character and medical skills.

One of these witnesses was a doctor from Cedars-Sinai Hospital named Toby Baggins. He couldn't point to any specific errors I had made, but because Truman was paying him as an expert witness, he said vague things such as, "Not that Panvini didn't do anything wrong during the operation …" Baggins also indicated that a written statement that Truman had prepared, alleging that I did something wrong, was not actually his statement. This showed that Truman was falsifying documents in federal court for personal gains.

My eyes almost popped out of my head, though, when Baggins turned to address the jury directly, which was irregular enough. But then he told them, "You know, I wrote this book called *Penis Power*." He started trying to sell his book to the jury! "You can get it on Amazon.com. Look it up. *Penis Power*." I almost burst out laughing, right there in the courtroom. The man was serious, because he repeated himself to the jury: "You can get this on Amazon.com." I think he was lacking some bett cells with mild dementia. I couldn't believe the judge didn't just throw him off the stand, since the judge was snickering as well. I guess that was all Truman could come up with.

Truman presented another witness, a Dr. Dawson, who had absolutely no evidence to substantiate that I did anything wrong, or that I had in any way deviated from the standard of care. Listening to him, I couldn't even understand why he was up there.

The second lawyer at the malpractice trial was another doctor named Jordan Dames, who looked like he was at least 110 years old. My lawyer and I were laughing under our breath as we watched that man's performance. He shuffled and shook like he had Parkinson's disease, and he spoke … to … the … jury … like … this. Just waiting for him to get a sentence out could take all morning. The jury eventually started laughing to themselves as he talked, because he was going off on tangents that made no sense and had nothing to do with the case, all while speaking so slowly that you could fall asleep between words.

Truman's case was a loser from day one. It had initially been filed by a different lawyer, in December 2012, in Mohave County, Arizona. But that lawyer hadn't thought that it would stand up in court, so he sat on it. In fact, he sat on it so long that he died. In the wake of his death, his partner looked it over and agreed that the case had no merit and that the charges would inevitably be dismissed.

Truman heard about the case through Dr. Morelli, and in his zeal to pursue me—part of his work with Chelsea, Veronica Fischer, and the Morellis—he approached Mrs. Marin and her family, talking them into letting him sue me for everything I had. In their grief, they sought to blame someone, and Truman had them smelling money too, so they said yes.

Before it all ended, he had roped in not just the widow but also Marin's children. During the final court proceeding, one of Marin's sons, Craig, was called as a witness. The forensic pathologist had already testified, and Craig Marin said, on the witness stand, that he wanted to apologize to me. "This case should never have gone forward," he said. "Had we known any of this, I would never have sued him." Everyone else was still pushing the issue, though, because they'd been brainwashed by Truman.

Truman destroyed himself because he just kept pushing the envelope. He solicited the case, and he even solicited other patients to file lawsuits against me where he didn't take an active role, just so he could deny any conflict of interest charge. My malpractice attorney, Caleb Wilder, knew exactly what was going on, because Truman confided in him, revealing a lot of malicious thoughts and actions in the process. Wilder told me this personally.

My attorney actually tried to stop Truman, telling him, "I don't know how you think you're gonna get away with this. You're not dealing with this in a legal fashion. And there's definite conflict of interest here. You're being sued by Dr. Panvini, and you are suing Dr. Panvini for this case." Truman had also represented Dr. Morelli, whose wife was hired as an alleged paralegal and expert witness (although she had absolutely no legal or medical background). So how do you get rid of the conflict of interest here?

Nothing would dissuade Truman, though. He continued to file and file and file. My lawyer said to him, "Listen, Connor, I don't want to have to be on the other side of a courtroom to testify against you. You should stop this immediately." But Truman just wouldn't listen.

Finally I'd had enough. When the jury verdict in the final case came back unanimously in my favor, I turned to my attorney and said, "We're going to get this guy." We had already begun the process of suing Connor Truman for malicious prosecution and abuse of process.

CHAPTER TWENTY-EIGHT

The Backfire

I had finally had enough. I had been the target of one attack after another for more than a decade, ever since Chelsea filed for divorce. First it was her and Veronica Fischer, then Dr. Morelli and his wife, then Truman, and finally all of them together coming after me. My life had been threatened and they had attempted to drive me out of my chosen profession, ruin my reputation, seize all my assets, and even forbid me from defending myself or escaping them by fleeing the country. They wanted to destroy me, but I had finally had enough.

When he repeatedly accused me of the murder of Albert Marin, an eighty-one-year-old man with multiple life-threatening health conditions who died, not because of anything I did, but in spite of my best efforts to save him, Connor Truman had gone too far. He had to be punished.

Our first move was to file a motion for summary judgment against Truman and the Marin family. They had already lost one previous round of summary judgment, when they attempted to charge that the nursing staff at Canyon Meadows Medical Center were negligent. They had failed to produce any experts who could testify to that imagined negligence, though, so the judge had thrown their case out. Similarly, they had no evidence that I was guilty of malpractice, so there was no reason to proceed to a trial.

The US District Court judge, H. Russel Holland, agreed, writing, "The motion is granted as to plaintiffs' claims based on allegations that Dr. Panvini negligently performed Mr. Marin's surgery. These claims are dismissed with prejudice." Dismissal with prejudice means that the person who brought the action is barred from bringing any other action based on the same claim. Truman could never again charge me in court with medical malpractice related to that man's tragic death.

We went to trial against Truman in July 2018. It was a three-day civil trial in Arizona. I sued him for malicious prosecution and abuse of process. These two things are closely related, but they differ in important and fundamental ways. Malicious prosecution is defined as intentionally (and maliciously) pursuing a legal action that was brought without probable cause and dismissed in favor of the person being prosecuted. Abuse of process, on the other hand, requires the plaintiff (that was me) to prove the existence of an ulterior purpose or motive for the legal charge, and some improper act in the use of the legal process during the prosecution of the case.

I had evidence for both of those charges. The summary judgment proving that I had not been negligent in my treatment of Mr. Marin was proof of malicious prosecution, and Truman had demonstrated abuse of process by chasing me from state to state and court to court with the same false, unprovable charges. In fact, he revealed in a letter to my attorney at the time, Caleb Wilder, that he was pursuing certain charges in Arizona rather than Nevada specifically because Nevada limited damages for negligence to $350,000, whereas Arizona had no cap. It was literally about nothing more than greed!

Truman's greed and ineptitude went even deeper than that. My attorney tried to warn him off, writing to him all the way back in 2013, "As you conceded when we met in person, your representation of Dr. Morelli, Dr. Panvini's ex-wife, and Mrs. Marin in separate proceedings represents a conflict of interest for you … Again, you have to make your own professional decisions and proceed in the manner you think best. But I did want to have a clear record that I have advised you of what I view to be significant conflict of interest problems."

Truman ignored this advice and pursued these cases for years, despite a total lack of evidence, maliciously inflating the charges far past the point where any judge or jury would have taken them—or him—seriously. In the process, he exploited his clients' vulnerable emotions, appealed to their greed, and ultimately conned them into joining him in a false and defamatory legal action.

Caleb Wilder was a tall, debonair man with a muscular build and a goatee. He came from a military background, and his sons followed his example; one son is now serving in the military in a Panama City beach in Florida. He had the sharpest mind of any attorney that I've ever met.

Wilder was one of the star witnesses at the trial. He knew everything about Truman's malicious intent, as expressed not only in letters but in private discussions between the two of them. My other major witness was Mrs. Marin, the dead man's widow, who had admitted on the stand that there was no basis for the charges and that they should never have attacked me in that way. Mrs. Marin admitted that she didn't think I was responsible for her husband's death.

There really was almost nothing for the jury to think about. The majority of the case had already been decided by the judge when I won the summary judgment, and it was agreed that the case met all the criteria for malicious prosecution and abuse of process. What the jury had to do was basically decide if they agreed with the judge, and if they did, how much did they want to award me?

Truman himself showed up in court wearing a black silk suit, white tie, and black shoes with white tops. He looked like a gangster, and it was obvious from their demeanor in the box that the jury did not like him. He defended himself, apparently forgetting the old saying, "A man who is his own lawyer has a fool for a client."

Even with all the time I'd spent around the man over the years, in depositions and lawyers' offices and various courtrooms, he still found a way to surprise me. It was a short trial, only three days, but midway through, he seemed to realize that he wasn't going to win, so he decided to throw everybody else under the bus. He claimed that it was the Morellis who had done all those terrible things to me, not him. He was just a pawn in their conspiracy.

"Yeah, but you hired her," my lawyer countered, referring to Truman's employment of Margaret as a paralegal and expert witness, despite her total lack of legal or medical expertise.

Truman had no way of evading that charge, so he said, "Well, I was hired by Veronica Fischer and Chelsea Panvini to do this. They should be held accountable."

Every time something he had done was brought up before the jury, Truman's response was, "Oh, that was Margaret and Dr. Morelli's doing." According to him, it had been their idea to contact my family; to send letters to the judge saying that I was a criminal; to argue that I should not have had the marijuana issue from Indiana expunged from my record; to file complaints with the Nevada Medical Licensing Board and the Arizona Medical Licensing Board; and to send defamatory letters to HIPAA, the Department of Health and

Human Services, and JCAHO stating that I had murdered Mr. Marin.

I was the chair of surgery at Canyon Meadows Medical Center, so I was privy to all this information because people in the administration who sympathized with me leaked it to me. Without some of those people, I might never have known the depths of the conspiracy against me.

If you have read this far, you have probably realized that I don't have much respect for the legal profession. However, during all of the false malpractice proceedings that Connor Truman launched against me, from convincing Emily Pitt to file a fraudulent claim against me to three separate cases regarding Mr. Marin, I was represented by a fabulous attorney by the name of Caleb Wilder. In my lifetime, more than a dozen attorneys have represented me on various issues, but three have truly stood out for their superb ethical and moral values. One was Caleb Wilder, and the others were Travis Abbott and Roy Ardent.

Caleb Wilder was on Connor Truman's back every step of the way during these phony malpractice cases. As I have described, he repeatedly warned Truman about making unprovable allegations that I had murdered my own patient. Truman never had any evidence to back up any of his claims, which put him in fundamental violation of Rule 11.

At one point, Wilder even told Truman, "Listen, you better retract your allegations, because I don't want to have to be on the witness stand testifying against you one day."

Truman replied, "I'm not worried. I like to have my cake and eat it at the same time."

Wilder told him, "You're making a big mistake, and you're going to regret this."

Again Truman had responded, in a cavalier fashion, that he wasn't worried.

Well, Wilder did ultimately find himself on the stand, testifying against Connor Truman. By then I was being represented by Travis Abbott, Wilder stated bluntly on the stand, "This was the most bizarre malpractice case that I had ever encountered in my entire career. Truman had absolutely no evidence to substantiate any of his claims, and he had violated Rule 11. And for the jury understanding, this is a rule that is standard in a courtroom proceeding that you must have unequivocal evidence before you make allegations in a formal lawsuit filing. Truman never had any evidence to file such malicious lawsuit claims."

As Wilder went on to testify, he said, "I've represented many doctors in malpractice cases, and one of the main issues and concerns that I had was that doctors accused of these type of malpractice charges are frequently suicide risks." He asserted that after Truman's relentless attacks against me, he had become concerned that I might one day take my own life. "The fact that Dr. Panvini is still here in the courtroom," he said, "says a lot about his integrity and his strength as a human being, that he can withstand all of this punishment."

Wilder said that I had never committed malpractice in my thirty-year career, and that the actions of Connor Truman were the worst that he had ever witnessed in his life.

The judge informed the jury of his findings on the summary judgment and told them the following:

> This court has already found that the defendants Connor Truman et al. have committed malicious prosecution; that Dino Panvini has already proven that defendants Mr. Truman et al. initiated or took active part in the prosecution of three civil proceedings against plaintiff Dino Panvini; that those actions terminated in Dino Panvini's favor; that the defendants acted without probable cause; and that the defendants acted with malice.

> The defendants' malicious prosecution is shown by the repeated initiation of lawsuits against plaintiff based on their unsupported belief that plaintiff willfully and maliciously caused the death of his own patient. The defendants' malice is evident in both the nature and number of repeated allegations.

Dino Panvini must prove defendants' malicious conduct was a cause of injury, damage, loss, or harm to Dino Panvini.

This court has already found the defendants Connor Truman et al. liable for abuse of process. The defendants willfully used against Dino Panvini the filing and service of three lawsuits against him and other procedures authorized by the court which are incident to the litigation process. Defendants used that process in a wrongful manner that was not proper in the regular course of proceedings; and defendants used that process primarily for an improper purpose or ulterior motive. You are asked to determine whether the wrongful use of that process caused injury, damage, loss, or harm to Dino Panvini.

The court has already found that the abuse of process was not reasonably justifiable in light of the legitimate litigation goals and can be logically explained only by improper purpose or ulterior motive, even if it was actually undertaken with bad intentions such as spite, ill will, or an intent to harass.

The court has also found that defendants used the process primarily for an improper purpose or ulterior motive, instead of the purpose for which the process was intended or authorized.

A primary improper purpose or ulterior motive requires more than an incidental motive or ill will to the plaintiff or benefit to the defendant, or an awareness that the action, through otherwise proper, will cause the opposing party to incur additional legal expenses or other injury.

You must decide the full amount of money that will be reasonable and fairly compensate plaintiff Dino Panvini for each of the following elements of damages proved by the evidence to have resulted from the defendants' malicious prosecution and abuse of legal process:

1. The expense that Dino Panvini has reasonably incurred in defending himself from the accusations and proceedings.

2. The harm to Dino Panvini's reputation resulting from the accusations brought against them from any defamatory matter alleged as a basis of the proceedings.

3. His emotional distress resulting from the bringing of the proceedings.

4. Any specific monetary loss that has resulted to him from the proceedings.

5. Lost earnings to date and any decrease in earning power or capacity in the future.

Total or partial compensation for injury which the injured party receives from a collateral source wholly independent of the wrongdoer does not operate to reduce the damages recoverable from the wrongdoer. In other words, even if the legal expenses caused to Dino Panvini by the malicious prosecution are covered by an insurer, he can nonetheless claim and recover compensation for their value from the defendants.

The case is now submitted for your decision. When you go to the jury room, you will choose a foreman. He or she will preside over your deliberations.

At least six of you must agree on a verdict. If all eight agree on a verdict, only the foreman need sign on the line marked "Foreman.. If six or seven agree on a verdict, all those who agreed, and only those who agree, must sign the verdict on the number of lines provided, leaving the line marked "Foreman" blank. Please print your name under your signature.

You will be given one form for the verdict; it reads as follows:

We the jury, duly impaneled and sworn in above-entitled cause, do find as follows:

_____ We assess damages in favor of plaintiff against Connor Truman and Connor Truman ESQ limited in the following amounts:

$_____ in damages, and

$_____ in punitive damages.

Or

_____We assess no damages against Connor Truman and Connor Truman ESQ limited.

Finally, all the witnesses had been questioned, all the arguments made, and the judge sent the jury out to deliberate. They were back in an hour. I watched their faces as they came in, and I knew they were on my side, but I couldn't believe what I heard when the verdict was announced.

As the jury entered the court, there was total silence in anticipation of what was to come. The foreman stood up and announced their verdict in my favor.

"We award Dino Panvini $6,232,000 for damages" to his reputation, employment, and business interests, and "We award Dino Panvini $1,768,000 in punitive damages." I glanced over at Truman, who was slumped in his chair with his hands over his face, as if he were thinking, *Oh my God, what have I done?* The jury awarded me a total of $8 million.

My heart was racing, and I couldn't believe what I was hearing. Finally, after all those years, justice was being served to those criminals!

Amazingly, after everything was over and the judge had dismissed the jury, Truman came over to me and tried to shake my hand. It was as if I had just beaten him in a country club tennis match, rather than finally defeating him after five years of legal combat.

I just looked at him without saying a word, but I had daggers in my eyes. I thought, *You son of a bitch, the audacity you have to attempt to extend your hand to me, you bastard.* I had such hatred for him, and I still do.

Interestingly, Truman told my lawyer, Caleb Wilder, "It's time for me to retire, because this case has taken a lot out of me." If someone is planning to retire, doesn't that suggest that they've accumulated a good nest egg? Truman recently claimed that he's broke and won't be able to pay the judgment. He hasn't obtained a bond that would protect him from my going after his assets, nor has he filed an official appeal—just an intent to appeal. So my attorneys are going after his assets, which is perfectly legal. I know for a fact that Truman has money in banks overseas, and I want him to commit perjury when my lawyers ask him about his finances. The chess game continues, but I'm a good chess player and I always go for checkmate!

The award was the largest in Mohave County history and even in the state of Arizona. After the trial, my attorney told the press,

> There was never any basis for the lawyer Connor Truman to claim that Dr. Panvini effectively murdered his patient. What the lawyer claimed in his lawsuit was that Dr. Panvini intentionally and maliciously caused the death of his own patient ... Even the lawyer's own client—the deceased patient's wife—admitted that she never believed that Dr. Panvini did that. The verdict is against the lawyer and his firm for filing a malicious lawsuit without probable cause and for abusing the legal system. I basically told the jury to let the patient's wife off the hook after she testified that she relied on her lawyer and that he didn't fully explain what he was doing to her.

Truman has signaled his intent to appeal the verdict, and he's attempting to hide his assets and plead poverty so he won't have to pay me. He's also been lucky that the Nevada Bar Association has declined to take action against him. I filed a complaint against him in 2013 when he started his malicious campaign, and the bar did absolutely nothing. Then I filed a follow-up, notifying them that he had been found guilty and informing them of the $8 million verdict against him. They responded with a one-paragraph letter that read as follows:

A Screening Panel of the Southern Nevada
Disciplinary Board reviewed the above-
referenced grievance file stemming from
your complaint concerning attorney Connor
Truman. The Panel concluded that formal
disciplinary proceedings would not be initiated
against the attorney. Accordingly, this grievance
has been dismissed and the file has been closed.

The American Bar Association obviously does not police
its own members, no matter how criminal. Lawyers have a
license to ruin anybody's reputation or destroy anybody's
career, and that's exactly what they've done, in case after
case, with mine being just one example. If any organization
needs to be policed and cleaned up, it's the American Bar
Association.

A complaint about a doctor is handled quite differently. For
example, when Chelsea dragged me into her marijuana issue,
my license was summarily suspended, because I was labeled "a
danger to society" until all the evidence was revealed. That's
what should have happened in this situation, but it never did.
The cases kept coming, but Truman knew that he wouldn't
be censured by his fellow lawyers. It was up to a jury to deliver
the punishment he deserved, but I still cannot understand
why he hasn't been disbarred.

Truman is now living the unexpected. Apparently he never
thought that the decision would be against him, especially for

such a large sum of money. He hasn't yet filed for a bond to prevent me from going after his assets. A bond of that nature would require 50 percent payment of the $8 million judgment, or $4 million. My lawyer is serving subpoenas to Truman to find out where his assets are hidden, including offshore accounts next month.

Truman's failure to disclose those offshore accounts can result in criminal penalties with IRS involvement. Right now Truman isn't accepting any subpoenas, and he's dodging the servers that we've hired in Nevada. This has necessitated us to hire counsel in Nevada, along with my attorneys in Arizona, to not only subpoena his assets but to also to go after his assets, especially since he isn't protecting his own butt!

Truman is now living the life that I lived for the past ten years. I'm sure he has seriously wished that he had never gotten involved with me in the first place. And I'm sure that he has thrown obscenities at Chelsea and her lawyer, asking them why the hell they got him into this. He just didn't know how relentless I can be, or that I would pursue him to the ends of the earth. You can run, but you cannot hide.

In Europe, when someone is sued for fraudulent or malicious actions and the patient or plaintiff loses, the Doctor is able to sue the lawyer who took the case, as well as the plaintiff, and automatically win, which is basically what has happened in this case. We need a similar process in the United States, to prevent frivolous, fraudulent malpractice suits and eliminate the enormous waste in the court system from such lawsuits. This would undoubtedly also reduce the cost of malpractice insurance, which now is astronomical. Unfortunately, there is a conflict of interest because most of our elected representatives in Washington, DC, are lawyers. We need to reestablish a proper balance in society, and as Washington says, "It's time to drain the swamp."

The years-long barrage of lawsuits filed by Truman and the relentless actions by Veronica Fischer, my ex-wife, and her co-conspirators have ruined my reputation. I have been unable to obtain employment by any hospital because of all the garbage that they falsely propagate.

Additionally, although I have filed whistleblower claims against doctors and hospitals, it is unlawful for the medical corporations that own them to show prejudice against me in obtaining privileges or employment in any of their hospitals. When I apply to any of the hospitals that they own, they reply with enthusiasm at first, but then I never get any further response because I've been blackballed. These large corporate hospitals have defied the qui tam laws intended to protect whistleblowers. These corporations began to thrive during the Clinton era when Hillary Clinton helped to establish the concept of managed care.

These hospitals don't care about patients; they only care about their corporate profits. In a community-owned hospital, profits are put back into the facility to improve patient care and safety. But in these large corporations, the CEOs get large stipends that go into their pockets, not back into patient care.

This illustrates how corrupt this whole system is, as it was initially created by Clinton. These large corporations are driving up costs and feeding greedy malpractice lawyers to the point of absurdity, and American people can't afford to pay. When I first started practicing medicine in 1987, there was Medicare and major medical with Blue Cross Blue Shield, but the patients would pay for their health care and then get reimbursed by their insurance companies.

Things have changed drastically since that time, and only for the worse. The good news is that the present administration is trying to break up this monopoly by opening up health care insurance so that policies can be sold across state lines. This form of competition is healthy and may drive down costs in the future.

The corruption within the legal system has been well documented. Lawyers file frivolous, fraudulent lawsuits for their own personal gain, which drives up health care costs as well as the price of malpractice insurance for doctors and hospitals.

My own inability to attain employment, however, can be traced directly back to Veronica Fischer and Connor Truman, who have relentlessly supported my wife's goal of destroying me. I know this because Chelsea said that directly to my father before he passed.

Still, my crusade for justice has not ended. I continue to pursue legal retribution from Chelsea and her former attorney,

Veronica Fischer, for everything they have done to ruin my life, and I am preparing to file charges against them.

But I will end my story for now with a warning: The American legal system doesn't work to protect the innocent or punish the guilty. It works to make money for lawyers. You enter courtrooms at your own peril.

As the old saying goes, what doesn't kill you makes you stronger. I'm now the strongest I've ever been in my life, both physically and emotionally. Remember, it's not over until it's over. I still need to collect the $8 million. Truman has been evading subpoenas from my attorneys and going into hiding. He claims that he has no money, but he was planning to retire. If that makes sense to anybody, please explain it to me. It's not rational to voluntarily retire without a large nest egg.

Victory is sweet, but final retribution is still the sweetest. Despite everything that I've been through over the past twelve years, writing this book has brought back many happy memories from the past. The Chinese have an old proverb: "With every catastrophe in life, there is an opportunity." My opportunity, now and in the near future, is to return to my profession of providing care to the sick and making them well again.

You might be wondering why I titled this book *The Medusa Enigma*. The word *medusa* represents the evil actions that originated with my ex-wife Chelsea and her collaborators, and *enigma* represents the convoluted issues that are part of this puzzle.

In the words of Vaclav Havel, "Hope is a state of mind, not of the world. Hope, in this deep and powerful sense, is not the same as joy that things are going well, or willingness to invest in enterprises that are obviously heading for success, but rather an ability to work for something because it is good, not because it stands for a chance to succeed."

As I've written this book, I've remembered the time when I died at the beginning of the book. I don't see that event as negative; in fact, it was a time when I underwent a metamorphosis, in May 2015, that transformed me into a more advanced form of myself. I'm stronger and more insightful, resilient, patient, and intuitive than ever before in my life. The series of events that I've related here has formed a new mycell or, more appropriately, a new pearl, in my memory bank.

All these actions have awakened a sleeping giant who still has much to do with his life, for which God has indisputably left me on this earth. Make no mistake, I have had to endure a lot of pain and suffering to get to the point where I am now, which has not only been a learning experience, but given me the awareness that there are no limits. As Louis Pasteur said, "Chance favors the prepared mind." All these events have conditioned me to be much more observant and prepared for the unexpected. Interestingly enough, since the events of my near-death experience I have developed a true sixth-sense where I am more perceptive and intuitive, when I encounter perplexing situations with more clarity. There are still many endeavors to be realized, and there is still justice to be served!

The only obstacles in life are the barriers we set up for ourselves. If you live with the understanding that you can achieve anything you want, there are no barriers. Never give up on something that you believe to be proper and ethical! The realization of our hopes and dreams comes only with persistence and determination to achieve the goals we set for ourselves. We must condition ourselves to remember that there are no limits to what we can accomplish. This will bring peace and harmony to your well-being, allowing you to attain anything you put your mind to. Speak softly but carry a big cane!

CPSIA information can be obtained
at www.ICGtesting.com
Printed in the USA
LVHW111452270919
632500LV00001B/81/P